EDUGORILLA
PUBLICATION

Computer Aptitude

For All Banking Mains Examinations

Latest Edition
Practice Kit

16 Tests
16 Topic-Wise Test

Topic Wise Chapters with Questions

✓ Thoroughly Revised and Updated

✓ Detailed Analysis of all MCQs

<table>
<tr><td>Title</td><td>: Computer Aptitude For All Banking Mains Examinations</td></tr>
<tr><td>Author Name</td><td>: Mr. Rohit Manglik</td></tr>
<tr><td>Published By</td><td>: EduGorilla Community Pvt. Ltd.</td></tr>
<tr><td>Publishers Address</td><td>: 12/651, First Floor Opp. Arvindo Park, Near Jama Masjid,
Indira Nagar, Lucknow, Uttar Pradesh-226016, India</td></tr>
</table>

Copyright EduGorilla

Disclaimer EduGorilla

Compiled and created by EduGorilla Community Pvt. Ltd

Printed By EduGorilla Community Pvt. Ltd.

ROHIT MANGLIK
CEO, EduGorilla

Dear Applicants,

People say *"Success comes to those who work hard."* But I've seen people working hard for their exams day in and day out for marginal success. While others succeed in their examinations by putting in just half the work. So are they God Gifted? No! I believe that it's because they work *smart* and not just *hard*. Similarly, for your exams, you should strategize your preparation so as to increase the likelihood of success. Well with EduGorilla get ready to increase your *chances of selection* in your exam by *16x*.

EduGorilla helps you in not only working *hard* but also working in a *smart and strategic* manner. With EduGorilla's preparation package, you get a chance to make your exam preparation easy, and a fun learning path towards selection. Finding the right path to your preparations can be difficult if you don't know in which direction to head. Don't worry, we have you covered! EduGorilla will be your guide to success in your journey. With our Preparation Package, you can prepare strategically and beat the exam in just one attempt.

EduGorilla's Preparation Package includes-

• **Test Series**   • **Books**

Our preparation package is handcrafted as per the latest changes, expert opinions, and students' discretion. Thus, enabling you to get through each stage of the selection process for your exam.

Our Books are designed by the teachers and experts of the respective exam with a combined 150+ years of experience; to provide you with easy, efficient, and effective learning. Our books are smart, in the sense that not only do they give you the answers to the questions but also provide similar questions for practice.

EduGorilla's competent Test Series gives you real-time experience and confidence through which you can clear your offline or online exam in just one attempt. We currently host 83,000+ mock tests for 1,440+ competitive and academic exams.

Thus, EduGorilla misses no chance to assist you in your preparation and covers all stages of the exam, so that you don't have to look anywhere else.

We provide complete preparation packages for defense, banking, teaching, and other National & State-Level exams. Hence, it doesn't matter which exam you aspire to because you will reach your success.

ALL THE BEST !

Let EduGorilla be your Guide to Success.

Rohit Manglik,
Founder and CEO, EduGorilla

INTRODUCTION

EduGorilla focuses on guiding students to succeed in their examinations. With that in mind, our book, titled "Computer Aptitude : For All Banking Mains Examinations", has been drafted through the collective efforts of our distinguished experts with 150+ years of combined experience. This book consists of questions that are created following the latest changes in the syllabus and exam pattern. We compiled the book on the basis of questions that are most likely to appear in the Banking Exams. Through EduGorilla's "Computer Aptitude : For All Banking Mains Examinations" your chances of success will increase 16x.

EduGorilla does this through our Complete Preparation Package. This package consists of well-conceptualized and structured content in the form of questions that are tailor-made according to your needs and will help you practice for exams in a smart way by pinpointing all the necessary information. It also provides hints and solutions, along with a smart answer sheet for your self-evaluation. You can assess your shortcomings and work accordingly on areas that may require more of your attention.

EduGorilla promises to help you succeed in your examination and accomplish your dream goals. We believe in our aspirants and see them at the top of the merit list. And the first step towards the top is to start preparing with us. EduGorilla's "Computer Aptitude : For All Banking Mains Examinations" includes the following attributes.

➤ Well-Researched Content

➤ Top-Notch Quality

➤ Detailed Answers and Analysis

➤ Smart Answer Sheet

➤ Exam Relevant Questions

Therefore, EduGorilla fortifies your preparation and makes it durable enough to help you stand tall and beat the examination.

TABLE OF CONTENTS

Q.1 What is the reason for avoiding the attributes property in the HTML DOM?

A. Found unnecessary
B. Attributes don't have attributes
C. Attributes have attributes
D. Considered irrelevant
E. None of the above

Q.2 In HTML, _______ attribute is used for merging of two or more adjacent columns.

A. CELLPADDING
B. CELLSPACING
C. ROWSPAN
D. COLSPAN
E. Both (A) and (B)

Q.3 Which of the following is a back-end language?

A. HTML
B. CSS
C. JavaScript
D. Python
E. None of these

Q.4 Which one is a web browser?

A. Facebook
B. Outlook express
C. Internet Explorer
D. Hotmail
E. Instagram

Q.5 Which component of MVC architecture deals the database?

A. View
B. Model
C. Controller
D. Storage
E. None of the above

Q.6 What are <a> and </a> tags used for?

A. Adding Image
B. Aligning text
C. Audio-voiced text
D. Adding links to your page
E. video-text

Q.7 Which is the correct HTML to left-align the contents inside a cell?

A. <tdleft>
B. <td ralign = "left">
C. <td align = "left">
D. <td leftalign>
E. None of the above

Q.8 Which of the following is/are true about proxy server?

I. HTTP doesn't support proxy server.

II. Proxy sever increases the load on original server.

A. Only I
B. Only II
C. Both I and II
D. Neither I nor II
E. None of these

Q.9 Which of the following is used to retrieve the information through URL (e.g. http://XYZ.com) on the world wide web?

A. Web server
B. client
C. Web browser
D. cookie
E. Web page

Q.10 Choices in DTD can be specified by using the ______ symbol.

A. |
B. OR
C. ||
D. ALTERNATIVE
E. All of the above

Q.11 In CSS, what is the correct syntax to add a background color for the body?

A. <body style ="background-color:lightgreen;">
B. <body style="bg-color:lightgreen;">
C. <body bg-color ="lightgreen;">
D. <body ="background-color:lightgreen;">
E. <body style-color ="lightgreen;">

Q.12 What is the correct HTML code for inserting an image?

A. <img> image.gif </img>
B. <img href="image.gif"/>
C. <img src="image.gif">
D. Both (A) and (B)
E. None of above

Q.13 While working on a JavaScript project, in your JavaScript application, which function would you use to send messages to users requesting for text input?

A. display()
B. prompt()
C. alert()
D. getInput()
E. None of these

Q.14 In HTML, from which tag descriptive tag starts?

A. <LL>
B. <DD>
C. <DL>
D. <DS>
E. <DA>

Q.15 If a web programmer is asked to make unordered list that has its item with circle, then which of the below given tag will be used to fulfill the need?

A. <ul style="style-type:circle">
B. <ul style="list-type:circle">
C. <ul style="list-style:circle">
D. <ul style="list-style-type:circle">
E. <ul style="type-style-list:circle">

Q.16 Which of the following is/are not true for HTML?

I. Head tags are not case sensitive.

II. Browsers displays the HTML tags.

A. Only I
B. Only II
C. Both I and II
D. Either I or II
E. None of these

Q.17 In CSS, how do you make each word in a paragraph start with a capital letter?

Example:

If input is "virat kohli is good cricket player." the output will be "Virat Kohli Is Good Cricket Player."

A. text-font: uppercase

B. text-transform: uppercase
C. text-transform: capitalize
D. text-font: capitalize
E. text-uppercase: capitalize

Q.18 Which of the following in not an open source web server?
A. Apache Tomcat　　　**B.** Nginx
C. Apache HTTP sever　　**D.** Microsoft IIS
E. None of these

Q.19 Find which "EduGorilla" text will be largest?
A. <h5> EduGorilla </h5>=
B. <h1> EduGorilla </h1>
C. <h2> EduGorilla </h2>
D. <h6> EduGorilla </h6>
E. <h4> EduGorilla </h4>

Q.20 Which tag is used to define a section in an HTML document?
A. <sec>　　**B.** <div>　　**C.** <td>　　**D.** <col>
E. <co>

Q.21 HTML stands for -
A. HighText Machine Language
B. HyperText and links Markup Language
C. HyperText Markup Language
D. HyperText Machine Language
E. None of these

Q.22 Which of the following tag is used to insert a line-break in HTML?
A.
　　B. <a>　　**C.** <pre>　　**D.** <b>
E. <bb>

Q.23 How to create an unordered list (a list with the list items in bullets) in HTML?
A. <ul>　　**B.** <ol>　　**C.** <li>　　**D.** <i>
E.

Q.24 How to create an ordered list (a list with the list items in numbers) in HTML?
A. <ul>　　**B.** <ol>　　**C.** <li>　　**D.** <i>
E. <pre>

Q.25 In HTML5, which of the following tag is used to initialize the document type?
A. <Doctype HTML>　　**B.** <\Doctype html>
C. <Doctype>　　**D.** <!DOCTYPE html>
E. None of these

Q.26 Which of the following tag is used to make the underlined text?
A. <i>　　**B.** <ul>　　**C.** <u>　　**D.** <pre>
E. <dr>

Q.27 How to create a checkbox in HTML?
A. <input type = "checkbox">
B. <input type = "button">
C. <checkbox>
D. <input type = "check">

E. None of these

Q.28 Which of the following tag is used to define options in a drop-down selection list?
A. <select>　　　　**B.** <list>
C. <dropdown>　　**D.** <option>
E. <input>

Q.29 Which of the following tag is used to add rows in the table?
A. <td> and </td>　　**B.** <th> and </th>
C. <tr> and </tr>　　**D.** Both (A) and (B)
E. None of the above

Q.30 The <hr> tag in HTML is used for-
A. new line　　　　**B.** vertical rule
C. new paragraph　　**D.** horizontal rule
E. None of the above

// Smart Answer Sheet //

| Correct | Percentage of students who answered correctly. | Skipped | Percentage of students who skipped. |

Q.	Ans.	Correct / Skipped	Q.	Ans.	Correct / Skipped	Q.	Ans.	Correct / Skipped	Q.	Ans.	Correct / Skipped	Q.	Ans.	Correct / Skipped	Q.	Ans.	Correct / Skipped
1	B	48.42 % / 43.16 %	6	D	85.75 % / 10.31 %	11	A	77.49 % / 12.73 %	16	B	44.41 % / 54.25 %	21	C	86.77 % / 10.76 %	26	C	89.27 % / 10.58 %
2	D	88.16 % / 11.08 %	7	C	82.03 % / 10.95 %	12	C	87.15 % / 12.59 %	17	C	56.03 % / 36.82 %	22	A	82.41 % / 16.31 %	27	A	81.02 % / 10.77 %
3	D	82.86 % / 16.83 %	8	D	48.95 % / 49.41 %	13	B	43.52 % / 30.42 %	18	D	59.94 % / 35.6 %	23	A	77.16 % / 11.42 %	28	D	82.32 % / 10.38 %
4	C	88.43 % / 10.47 %	9	C	89.95 % / 10.02 %	14	C	86.6 % / 12.03 %	19	B	81.44 % / 15.75 %	24	B	81.17 % / 10.76 %	29	C	87.39 % / 10.64 %
5	B	56.25 % / 30.98 %	10	A	46.58 % / 40.99 %	15	D	45.45 % / 53.77 %	20	B	84.8 % / 10.4 %	25	D	89.09 % / 10.55 %	30	D	84.04 % / 13.04 %

//Hints and Solutions//

1. When a web page is loaded, the browser creates a Document Object Model of the page. The reason for avoiding the attributes property in the HTML DOM is because Attributes don't have attributes.

The HTML DOM is a standard object model and programming interface for HTML. It defines:

- The HTML elements as objects
- The properties of all HTML elements
- The methods to access all HTML elements
- The events for all HTML elements.

Hence, the correct option is (B).

2. COLSPAN is the attribute of HTML language which defines the number of columns a table cell should span. It can be applied to <td> and <th>. HTML is a language that is used to create web pages and web applications. There are numbers of attributes in HTML language and COLSPAN is one of them.

Hence, the correct option is (D).

3. Python is a back-end language.

- Python is an interpreted, high-level, general-purpose programming language.
- Python can be used on a server to create web applications.
- Python lets user work quickly and integrate systems more efficiently.

Therefore, python is treated as a back-end language.

Notes: Although JavaScript can also be used as a back-end language.

Hence, the correct option is (D).

4. A browser is a software application used to locate, retrieve and display the content of Web pages, images, videos and other files. The browser contacts the Web server and requests information and the Web server sends the information back to the Web browser which displays the results on the computer.

Some commonly used web browsers are:

- **Internet Explorer**
- Firefox
- Google Chrome
- Opera
- Netscape

Hence, the correct option is (C).

5. Model–view–controller (MVC) is a software design pattern commonly used for developing user interfaces that divide the related program logic into three interconnected elements Model, View and Controller. But the Model element is deal with the database. Model is the central component of the architecture. It is the application's dynamic data structure, independent of the user interface. It directly manages the data, logic and rules of the application.

Hence, the correct option is (B).

6. <a> tag is used to add links to webpage.

The <a> tag defines a hyperlink, which is used to link from one page to another.

Attribute 'href' indicates the link's destination.

Hence, the correct option is (D).

7. The align attribute specifies the horizontal alignment of the content in a cell.

Syntax:

<td align="left ">

Attribute value left is default for <td>. It left-aligns content.

Hence, the correct option is (C).

8. Both statements are false.

- HTTP supports proxy servers.
- A proxy server is a computer that keeps copies of responses to recent requests. The HTTP client sends a request to the proxy server. The proxy server checks its cache. If the response is not stored in the cache, the proxy server sends the request to the corresponding server. Incoming responses are sent to the proxy server and stored for future requests from other clients.
- The proxy server reduces the load on the original server, decreases traffic, and improves latency. However, to use the proxy server, the client must be configured to access the proxy instead of the target server.

Hence, the correct option is (D).

9. Web browser is used to retrieve the information through URL (e.g. http://XYZ.com) on the world wide web. A web browser is a software application for accessing the information on the World Wide Web. URL is an acronym for Uniform Resource Locator, It is a reference to the resource on the internet.

Hence, the correct option is (C).

10. Choices in DTD can be specified by using the I symbol. DTD stands for document type definition. This defines the structure and attributes of an XML document.

Various elements are there in DTD. Some are choices, sequence, etc.

- **I** – choice operator
- **?** – this is the optional operator (zero or one time)
- ***** - this is zero to many operator
- **,** - sequence operator

Hence, the correct option is (A).

11. The CSS background-color property defines the background color for an HTML element

```
<html>
<body style ="background-color: lightgreen;">
<h1>Edugorilla Dashboard</h1>
<p>TESTSERIES</p>
</body>
</html>
```

Hence, the correct option is (A).

12. HTML code for inserting an image is `<img src="image.gif">`.

The `<img>` tag defines an image in an HTML page.

The `<img>` tag has two required attributes: src and alt.

src specifies the URL of an image and alt specifies an alternate text for an image.

Hence, the correct option is (C).

13. The prompt() method displays a dialogue box that prompts the visitor for input.

The below statement will ask the user to input his/her test series and the default value is EduGorilla.

Code:

```
var favDrink = prompt("Which test series you are taking?", "EduGorilla");
```

Hence, the correct option is (B).

14. HTML Description List or Definition List displays elements in definition form like in dictionary. The `<dl>`, `<dt>` and `<dd>` tags are used to define description list.

The 3 HTML description list tags are given below:

- `<dl>` tag defines the description list.
- `<dt>` tag defines data term.
- `<dd>` tag defines data definition (description).

Hence, the correct option is (C).

15. If a web programmer is asked to make an unordered list that has its item with the circle, then `<ul style="list-style-type:circle">` tag will be used. An unordered list typically is a bulleted list of items. HTML 3.0 gives you the ability to customise the bullets, to do without bullets and to wrap list items horizontally or vertically for multicolumn lists.

Hence, the correct option is (D).

16. Head tag names for HTML elements may be written with any mix of lowercase and uppercase letters that are a case-insensitive match for the names of the elements given in the HTML elements section; that is, tag names are case-insensitive. So, the statement I is true. Browsers do not display HTML tags. It displays the HTML document. So, statement II is not true.

Hence, the correct option is (B).

17. In CSS, to make each word in a paragraph start with a capital letter we will use text-transform: capitalize. text-transform property controls the capitalization of text.

Code for the given example:

```
<html>
<head>
<style>
div.c {text-transform: capitalize;}
</style>
</head>
<body>
<div class="c">virat kohli is good cricket player.</div>
</body>
</html>
```

Output:

Virat Kohli Is Good Cricket Player.

Hence, the correct option is (C).

18. Internet Information Server (IIS) is not open-source software. IIS is a flexible, general-purpose webserver from Microsoft that runs on Windows systems to serve requested HTML pages or files. An IIS web server accepts requests from remote client computers and returns the appropriate response. IIS supports HTTP, HTTP/2, HTTPS, FTP, FTPS, SMTP and NNTP.

Hence, the correct option is (D).

19.

- The `<h1>` to `<h6>` tags are used to define HTML headings.
- `<h1>` defines the most important heading. `<h6>` defines the least important heading.
- h1 is a largest heading and h6 is a smallest heading
- It has a start tag `<h1>` and an end tag `</h1>`.

So, `<h1>` Edugorilla `</h1>` will largest text.

Hence, the correct option is (B).

20. `<div>` tag defines a division or a section in an HTML document.

The `<div>` element is often used as a container for other HTML elements to style them with CSS or to perform certain tasks with JavaScript.

Hence, the correct option is (B).

21. HTML stands for HyperText Markup Language, which is used for creating web pages and web applications.

HyperText simply means "Text within Text." A text that has a link within it, is a hypertext. A markup language is a computer language that is used to apply layout and formatting conventions to a text document.

Hence, the correct option is (C).

22. The <br> tag in the HTML document is used to create a line break in a text. If we place the <br> tag in HTML code, then it works the same as pressing the enter key in a word processor.

Hence, the correct option is (A).

23. The <ul> tag in HTML is used to display the list items in a bulleted format. There can be three types of an unordered list: disc, circle and square.

- disc- Sets the list item marker to a bullet (default).
- circle- Sets the list item marker to a circle.
- square Sets the list item marker to a square.

Hence, the correct option is (A).

24. The <ol> tag in HTML is used to display the list items in a numbered format. There can be different types of numbered lists: Numeric numbers, uppercase alphabet, lowercase alphabet, uppercase roman number, lowercase roman number etc.

Numeric numbers	type="1"	The list items will be numbered with numbers (default)
uppercase alphabet	type="A"	The list items will be numbered with uppercase letters
lowercase alphabet	type="a"	The list items will be numbered with lowercase letters
uppercase roman number	type="I"	The list items will be numbered with uppercase roman numbers
lowercase roman number	type="i"	The list items will be numbered with lowercase roman numbers

Hence, the correct option is (B).

25. The <!DOCTYPE html> tag is used to inform the browser about the version of HTML used in the document. It is called as the document type declaration (DTD).

Hence, the correct option is (D).

26. The <u> (underline tag) tag in HTML is used to display the underlined text. It rendered as a solid underlined text, but it can be changed using CSS properties.

Hence, the correct option is (C).

27. To create a checkbox in HTML, we have to use the <input> tag and give the value checkbox to its type attribute. So, we are use <input type = "checkbox">.

Hence, the correct option is (A).

28. The <option> tag in HTML is used to define options in a dropdown list within <select> or <datalist> element. A dropdown list must have at least one <option> element.

Hence, the correct option is (D).

29. <tr> and </tr> tag is used to add rows in the table. The <tr> tag in HTML is used to define the rows in the table. It can consist one or more <th> head cells and <td> data cells to define a single row of HTML table.

Hence, the correct option is (C).

30. The <hr> tag in HTML stands for horizontal rule and is used to insert a horizontal rule or a thematic break in an HTML page to divide or separate document sections. The <hr> tag is an empty tag, and it does not require an end tag.

Hence, the correct option is (D).

Q.1 What is the full form of EEPROM?
A. Electronically Erasable Programmed Read-Only Memory
B. Easily Erasable Programmed Read-Only Memory
C. Electronically Erasable Programming Read-Only Memory
D. Electrically Erasable Programmable Read-Only Memory
E. None of these

Q.2 The Central Processing Unit (CPU) in a computer consists of:
A. Input, output and processing
B. Control unit, primary storage and secondary storage
C. Control unit, arithmetic-logic unit and primary storage
D. Control unit, arithmetic-logic unit and secondary storage
E. None of the above

Q.3 Which of the following is an output device?
A. MIC
B. Mouse
C. Speaker
D. Keyboard
E. Joystick

Q.4 The value of a Terabyte is:
A. 1024 Petabytes
B. 1024 Megabytes
C. 1024 Gigabytes
D. 1024 Kilobytes
E. None of the above

Q.5 ____is space between your content and the edge of the page in MS Excel.
A. Margin
B. Print Area
C. Orientation
D. Print titles
E. Layout

Q.6 The word 'Spam' is related to?
A. Computer
B. Arts
C. Music
D. Sports
E. Movie

Q.7 Which process checks to ensure the components of the computer are operating and connected properly?
A. Booting
B. Processing
C. Saving
D. Drafting
E. None of these

Q.8 Which one of the following computer components is faster in terms of speed of access?
A. USB Drive
B. Solid State Drive
C. RAM
D. Hard Disk Drive
E. ROM

Q.9 Virus is a program that has been written to interfere with the normal functioning of a computer. Which of the below in not a type of virus?

[UPSSSC Forest Guard, 2018]

A. Boot sector viruses
B. System viruses
C. File viruses
D. Disc viruses

E. Both (A) & (C)

Q.10 Which among the following is NOT an open source software?

[UPSSSC Forest Guard, 2018]

A. Linux
B. Microsoft Office
C. Mozilla Firefox
D. Android
E. All of the above

Q.11 What is the keyboard shortcut for 'Undo' function?

[UPSSSC Forest Guard, 2018]

A. Ctrl + Z
B. Ctrl + V
C. Ctrl + C
D. Ctrl + U
E. Ctrl + S

Q.12 The machine language of computer is based on:
A. Abstract Algebra
B. Matrix Algebra
C. Boolean Algebra
D. Linear Algebra
E. None of the above

Q.13 Which of the following programming languages are considered as low level languages?
A. Basic, Cobol, Fortran
B. C, C++
C. Assembly language
D. Prolog
E. Pascal

Q.14 What is the size of IPv4?
A. 8-bit
B. 16-bit
C. 32-bit
D. 64-bit
E. 58-bit

Q.15 Which is not a browser for surfing the Internet.
A. Internet Explorer
B. Opera
C. Mozilla Firefox
D. Google
E. All of these

Q.16 Name the memory that acts between the main memory and the Central processing unit?
A. Cache Memory
B. Register Memory
C. Virtual Memory
D. Both (B) & (C)
E. None of these

Q.17 Which of the following hardware device used for Printing vector graphics?
A. Ink jet Printer
B. Plotter
C. Keyboard
D. Mouse
E. Monitor

Q.18 What is the meaning of CAPTCHA used in computer terminology?
A. Control Automated Public Turing test to tell Computers and Humans Apart
B. Completely Automated Portal Turing test to tell Computers and Humans Apart
C. Completely Apprehensive Public Turing test to tell

Computer and Humans Apart

D. Completely Automated Public Turing test to tell Computers and Humans Apart

E. Control Automated Portal Turing test to tell Computers and Humans Apart

Q.19 Which among the following is NOT a database software in computers?

[UPSSSC Forest Guard, 2018]

A. MS Access   **B.** Foxpro
C. Oracle   **D.** MS Word
E. MySQL

Q.20 Which of the following factor does not makes effective and efficient Network?

A. Performance   **B.** Reliability
C. Server Load   **D.** Robustness
E. None of these

Q.21 What does Ctrl + = key effect in Microsoft Office?

A. Uppercase   **B.** Superscript
C. Subscript   **D.** Lowercase
E. None of these

Q.22 Networks that connects a group of computers in a small geographical area is called-

A. Local Area Network
B. Personal Area Network
C. Wide Area Network
D. Metropolitan Area Network
E. None of these

Q.23 With reference to the hardware parts in computers, what is the full form of VRAM?

A. Video Random Advanced Media
B. Video Random Access Memory
C. Versatile Read Access Memory
D. Versatile Read Advanced Media
E. Versatile Random Access Memory

Q.24 Which of the following statements is/are correct?

1. The purpose of the transmitter is to convert the message signal produced by the source of information into a form suitable for transmission through the channel.

2. The receiver reconstructs a recognizable form of the original message signal for delivering it to the user of information.

3. The channel is not the medium between the receiver and the transmitter.

A. 1 only   **B.** 2 only
C. Both 1 and 2   **D.** Only 3
E. Both 1 and 3

Q.25 POP3 and IMAP are e-mail accounts in which:

A. One automatically gets one's mail everyday
B. One has to be connected to the server to read or write one's mail
C. One only has to be connected to the server to send and receive e-mail
D. One does not need any telephone lines

E. None of these

Q.26 Which option is used in Ms-Word to make the formatting of even columns different from subject columns?

[Rajasthan Police Constable, 2020]

A. Banded Rows   **B.** First Column
C. Banded Column   **D.** Last Column
E. Middle Column

Q.27 Which of the following is an open source word processor ?

A. MS Word Online   **B.** Word Perfect Office
C. Kwrite   **D.** MS Excel
E. None of the above

Q.28 What is the easiest way to place same graphic in same place in all slides?

A. Place graphic in Slide Master
B. Place graphic in Notes Master
C. Place graphic manually in all slide
D. Place graphic in Handout Master
E. None of these

Q.29 In the Microsoft PowerPoint presentation, to select one hyperlink after another during a slide presentation, which of the following keyboard key is pressed?

A. Tab   **B.** Ctrl + K   **C.** Ctrl + H   **D.** F1
E. F2

Q.30 Microsoft Office is an example of which type of Software?
A. Vertical market software
B. Horizontal market software
C. Open software
D. Circuit market software
E. Closed software

// Smart Answer Sheet //

| Correct | Percentage of students who answered correctly. | Skipped | Percentage of students who skipped. |

Q.	Ans.	Correct / Skipped	Q.	Ans.	Correct / Skipped	Q.	Ans.	Correct / Skipped	Q.	Ans.	Correct / Skipped	Q.	Ans.	Correct / Skipped	Q.	Ans.	Correct / Skipped
1	D	49.87 % / 34.13 %	6	A	85.98 % / 13.99 %	11	A	84.84 % / 10.24 %	16	A	62.23 % / 32.5 %	21	C	68.56 % / 30.13 %	26	C	52.64 % / 34.88 %
2	C	42.86 % / 38.69 %	7	A	89.37 % / 10.11 %	12	C	67.97 % / 30.36 %	17	B	76.79 % / 17.54 %	22	A	41.42 % / 55.56 %	27	A	87.81 % / 10.51 %
3	C	82.18 % / 16.99 %	8	C	67.28 % / 30.24 %	13	C	59.56 % / 40.12 %	18	D	48.45 % / 45.25 %	23	B	60.74 % / 36.73 %	28	A	88.94 % / 10.6 %
4	C	76.79 % / 21.35 %	9	B	87.71 % / 11.64 %	14	C	51.35 % / 34.32 %	19	D	56.53 % / 39.19 %	24	C	24.22 % / 72.38 %	29	A	83.65 % / 11.97 %
5	A	55.84 % / 42.86 %	10	B	88.47 % / 11.39 %	15	D	68.86 % / 30.71 %	20	C	47.82 % / 30.95 %	25	C	24.28 % / 69.18 %	30	B	40.44 % / 45.7 %

//Hints and Solutions//

1. The full form of EEPROM is "Electrically Erasable Programmable Read-Only Memory". The EEPROM is a form of non-volatile memory where data can be erased and reprogrammed using an electrical charge.

Hence, the correct option is (D).

2. Control unit, arithmetic-logic unit, primary storage.

The Central Processing Unit (CPU), the principal part of any digital computer system, generally composed of the main memory, control unit, and arithmetic-logic unit.

It constitutes the physical heart of the entire computer system, it is linked to various peripheral equipment, including input/output devices and auxiliary storage units.

In modern computers, the CPU is contained on an integrated circuit chip called a microprocessor.

The control unit part controls the input and output devices.

Arithmetic-logic units do basic operations like addition, multiplication, and division.

A primary storage device is a medium that holds a memory for a short period of time while a computer is running.

Hence, the correct option is (C).

3. An output device is a piece of computer hardware that receives data from a computer and then translates that data into another form. That form may be audio, visual, textual, or hard copy such as a printed document.

The key distinction between an input device and an output device is that an input device sends data to the computer, whereas an output device receives data from the computer.

Computer speakers are hardware devices that transform the signal from the computer's sound card into audio. Speakers create sound using internal amplifiers that vibrate at different frequencies according to data from the computer. This produces sound.

Hence, the correct option is (C).

4. The smallest unit of memory is called a bit.

Bit stands for binary digit.

The memory of a computer is measured in Bytes

The storage capacity of a hard disk is measured in Megabytes, Gigabytes, and Terabytes.

The terabyte is a multiple of the unit byte for digital information.

The value of a Terabyte is 1024 Gigabytes.

1 TB = 1000000000000 bytes = 10^{12} bytes

Hence, the correct option is (C).

5. Margin is the space between your content and the edge of the page.

Margins are set to Normal, which is a one-inch space between the content and each edge of the page.

You may need to adjust the margins to make your data fit more comfortably on the page.

To better align an Excel worksheet on a printed page, you can change margins, specify custom margins, or centre the worksheet—either horizontally or vertically on the page.

Page margins are the blank spaces between your data and the edges of the printed page. Top and bottom page margins can be used for things such as headers, footers, and page numbers.

Hence, the correct option is (A).

6. Spam:

It is the use of messaging systems to send an unsolicited message to large numbers of recipients for the purpose of commercial advertising.

The term is applied to similar abuses in other media, Usenet newsgroup spam, instant messaging spam, Web search engine spam, spam in blogs, wiki spam, online classified ads spam, mobile phone messaging spam, Internet forum spam, junk fax transmissions, spam mobile apps, social spam, television advertising and file sharing spam.

Hence, the correct option is (A).

7. Alternatively referred to as boot-up or sometimes startup, booting is the process of powering on a computer and getting into the operating system.

During the boot process, the computer goes through multiple steps, to ensure the computer hardware works correctly, and the necessary software can be loaded.

Hence, the correct option is (A).

8. Memory in a computer system is required for the storage and retrieval of instructions and data. A system uses a variety of devices for storing these instructions and data that are required for its operation.

The following are the three kinds of Memory Systems:

1. Primary (main) Memory: Primary memories are used mainly for primary storage. It stores programs and data which are currently needed by the CPU. The primary memory is a static device. There is no rotating part in it. Examples include RAM, ROM, etc.

- Random Access Memory (RAM): It stores data that the computer needs to use temporarily. So it is faster in terms of accessibility compared to the secondary storage devices. It is a volatile memory i.e. the data disappear from it when the power is off.

- Read-Only Memory (ROM): The system uses ROM to boot itself. It is used to store the start-up information of the computer. This is called non-volatile memory i.e. it retains its content even if the computer loses its power.

- Cache Memory: It stores program instruction and data that the computer uses more frequently. The processor

can access this information from the cache rather than having to get it from the computer's main memory.

2. Secondary Memory: It is the storage that the CPU cannot access directly. t's content firstly needs to be copied into ram and then transferred to CPU. It stores data that can be easily retrieved only by the main memory and used by the processor. For example, hard disk.

3. Tertiary Memory: It includes a mechanism to insert and remove mass storage media into a storage device. It is useful for extensive data storage. For example, compact discs (CD) and USB drives.

So, as you can from the listed points, RAM is faster in terms of speed of access.

Hence, the correct option is (C).

9. System virus is not a type of virus.

Boot sector virus means that that affects the boot sector of the floppy disk.

It damages that portion of the computer which has critical information regarding the working of the computer's operating system.

File virus is a virus that infects executable files aiming to make permanent damage to the file or making it unusable.

Disc virus enters the computer if any infected external disk or floppy containing the virus is attached to the system.

All the computer viruses combined are called system viruses.

Hence, the correct option is (B).

10. Open-source software means the source code of the software is made available by the authors.

It is done so that people can view that code, learn from it, copy from it, alter it or share it with someone.

It is released with a license and the author holds its copyright.

The commonly used open-source software is Apache HTTP server, browsers like Mozilla Firefox, and Google Chrome Libreoffice.

One of the most successful open-source software is the Linux operating system.

Other examples include Android, Unix, Ubuntu, etc.

Hence, the correct option is (B).

11. Undo is a technique or a command which is implemented in many computer programs.

It erases the last change done to the document.

We can undo, redo, or repeat many actions in Microsoft Word, PowerPoint, and Excel.

With the help of undo command, the users can explore and work without fear of making mistakes, because changes can be made whenever required.

In Microsoft Windows applications, the keyboard shortcut for the Undo command is Ctrl+Z or Alt+Backspace, and the shortcut for Redo is Ctrl+Y or Ctrl+Shift+Z.

Hence, the correct option is (A).

12. The machine language of the computer is based on Boolean Algebra.

Abstract algebra is the set of advanced topics of algebra that deal with abstract algebraic structures rather than the usual number systems. The most important of these structures are groups, rings, and fields.

In Matrix Algebra, a matrix is a rectangular array or table of numbers, symbols, or expressions, arranged in rows and columns.

Boolean Algebra in mathematics and mathematical logic, Boolean algebra is the branch of algebra in which the values of the variables are the truth values true and false, usually denoted 1 and 0, respectively.

Linear algebra is the branch of mathematics concerning linear equations such as linear maps such as: and their representations in vector spaces and through matrices. Linear algebra is central to almost all areas of mathematics.

Hence, the correct option is (C).

13. Two common types of low-level programming languages are assembly language and machine language.

Examples of high-level programming languages in active use today include Python, Visual Basic, Delphi, Perl, PHP, ECMAScript, Ruby, C#, Java.

A software developer can create and edit source code in a high-level language using a programming IDE or even a basic text editor.

Hence, the correct option is (C).

14. IPv4 was the primary version of IP.

It was sent for creation in the ARPANET in 1983.

It is generally utilized IP adaptation.

The IPv4 uses a 32-bit address scheme.

IPv4 binary bits are separated by a dot(.)

IPv4 support broadcast.

IPv4 binary bits are a dot(.).

IPv4 security permits encryption to keep up privacy and security.

Hence, the correct option is (C).

15. Internet Explorer is a series of graphical web browsers and included in the Microsoft Windows line of operating systems.

It was developed by Microsoft and started in 1995.

Mozilla Firefox is a web browser developed by the Mozilla foundation.

Opera Browser is a web browser developed by Opera Software initially on 10th April 1995.

A gaming browser called Opera GX was launched on 11 June 2019.

Hence, the correct option is (D).

16. Cache Memory is a high-speed memory that acts as a buffer between RAM and the CPU.

It holds the data of the main memory that is used by the CPU frequently. The size of cache memory is smaller as compared to main memory.

Register memory is the smallest and fastest memory that temporarily holds the data and instructions that are used frequently by the CPU.

Virtual memory is a memory that enables a computer to compensate for the lack of physical memory. It allows users to store processes that are larger than the main memory available.

Hence, the correct option is (A).

17. The plotter is basically a type of Printer.

It is an output device of the computer.

It uses a pen to create a print on paper or media.

The output is created on vector graphics.

It means that the dots are printed which are joined by lines and curves to produce text and images.

Plotters are present in many designs used for printing large format prints.

It includes architecture like layouts, building plans, ship designs, CAD (computer-aided design), big canvas prints, and any other engineering drawing.

The plotters utilize pens or markers to draw graphics on an output media.

These pens move differently according to the technology deployed by a plotter.

Hence, the correct option is (B).

18. Captcha refers to the Completely Automated Public Turing Test to differentiate between computers and humans.

A Captcha Security Code is an image of letters that a person must type in to match the Captcha image they see.

It is a type of challenge-response test used in computing to ensure that the response is not generated by a computer.

This code was created to stop automated computer spam robots from filling out forms and harvesting email addresses and then sending out spam emails.

Only a human can type out a code he sees correctly, an automated computer programme cannot.

Hence, the correct option is (D).

19. MS Word since it's a word processor.

Microsoft Word is a word processor developed by Microsoft. It was first released on October 25, 1983, under the name Multi-Tool Word for Xenix systems.

Hence, the correct option is (D).

20. Server Load expresses how many processes are waiting in the queue to access the computer processor.

This is calculated for a certain period of time, and the smaller the number the better.

Hence, the correct option is (C).

21. In Microsoft Office, the effect of Ctrl + = key is Subscript.

A subscript is a character that is usually a number or a letter, a subscript is written below or below and to the right or left of another character.

Hence, the correct option is (C).

22. Networks that connect a group of computers in a small geographical area is called Local Area Network.

Local Area Network is used inside an office building or inside a classroom.

Ethernet and WiFi are the most common technologies used to build a Local Area Network.

Hence, the correct option is (A).

23. Computers generally have special video memory (VRAM) to hold graphical images, called bitmaps, for the computer display.

This memory is often dual-ported—a new image can be stored in it at the same time that its current data is being read and displayed.

Hence, the correct option is (B).

24. In a communication system, the transmitter is located at one place, the receiver is located at some other place (far or near) separate from the transmitter and the channel is the physical medium that connects them.

The purpose of the transmitter is to convert the message signal produced by the source of information into a form suitable for transmission through the channel.

The receiver reconstructs a recognizable form of the original message signal for delivering it to the user of information.

Hence, the correct option is (C).

25. POP3 and IMAP are e-mail accounts in which one only has to be connected to the server to send and receive e-mail.

- IMAP stands for Internet Message Access Protocol.
- POP3 stands for Post Office Protocol.

Hence, the correct option is (C).

26. Banded Column is used in Ms-Word to make the formatting of even columns different from subject columns.

Banding:

- Adding color to alternate rows or columns called banding.
- It can make the data in our worksheet easier to scan.

Hence, the correct option is (C).

27. MS Word Online is an open-source word processor.

Microsoft Word Online is a graphical word processing program that users can type with.

- It is made by Microsoft.
- Its purpose is to allow users to type and save documents.
- The most recent version is Word for Office 365.

Hence, the correct option is (A).

28. The easiest way to place the same graphic in the same place in all slides is to Place the graphic in Slide Master.

- Slide Master is a tool used in Microsoft PowerPoint to create slide templates.
- Slide Master can save slide layouts, including the background, color, fonts, effects, positioning, etc.

Hence, the correct option is (A).

29. In the Microsoft PowerPoint presentation, to select one hyperlink after another during a slide presentation, the Tab key is pressed.

Other keys:

Ctrl+K is used to Insert a hyperlink.

Ctrl + H is used to Edit or Replace.

F1 is used to open the Help panel.

F2 key is used to rename a highlighted icon, file or folder across all recent versions of Windows.

Hence, the correct option is (A).

30. Microsoft Office is an example of Horizontal market software.

- A Horizontal market is one that supplies goods to a variety of industries instead of just one.
- Therefore, Horizontal market software is software that can be used by several different types of industries.
- For example, word processing and spreadsheet programs are horizontal market applications because they can be used by many types of businesses and consumers.

Hence, the correct option is (B).

Q.1 Who developed the basic architecture of computers?

A. Blaise Pascal   **B.** Charles Babbage

C. John Von Neumann   **D.** Seymour Cray

E. None of these

Q.2 A processor performing fetch or decoding of different instruction during the execution of another instruction is called ______.

A. Super-scaling

B. Pipe-lining

C. Parallel Computation

D. Normal Scaling

E. None on the above

Q.3 The BUS busy line is used ________.

A. To indicate the processor is busy.

B. To indicate that the BUS master is busy.

C. To indicate the BUS is already allocated.

D. Both (A) and (B)

E. None of these

Q.4 A ______ circuit is a connected arrangement of logic gates with a set of inputs and outputs.

A. Arithmetic   **B.** Logic

C. Combinational   **D.** Shift

E. None of these

Q.5 Low level languages are also known as:

A. Sources code   **B.** Middle code

C. C Language   **D.** Machine Language

E. High-level language

Q.6 The interrupt servicing mechanism in which the requesting device identifies itself to the processor to be serviced is ________ .

A. Polling

B. Vectored interrupts

C. Interrupt nesting

D. Simultaneous requesting

E. None of these

Q.7 The sign magnitude representation of -1 is ________ .

A. 0001   **B.** 1110   **C.** 1000   **D.** 1001

E. 0000

Q.8 Which of the following circuit convert the binary data into a decimal?

A. Decoder   **B.** Encoder

C. Code converter   **D.** Multiplexer

E. None of these

Q.9 CPU performs ______ operation.

A. Data transfer

B. Logic operation

C. Arithmetic operation

D. I/O operation

E. All of the Above

Q.10 'IC chips' for computers are usually made of?

[MP Sub Inspector (MPSI), 2017]

A. Gold   **B.** Silicon

C. Lead   **D.** Chromium

E. Silver

Q.11 After the completion of the DMA transfer, the processor is notified by ________ .

A. Acknowledge signal

B. Interrupt signal

C. WMFC signal

D. Line

E. None of these

Q.12 If any one of the input is 1, then the gate that gives 1 output, is known as ______.

A. AND   **B.** NAND

C. OR   **D.** NOT

E. None of these

Q.13 8051 series has how many 16-bit registers?

A. 2   **B.** 3   **C.** 1   **D.** 0

E. 4

Q.14 To overcome the conflict over the possession of the BUS we use ______.

A. Optimizers

B. BUS arbitrators

C. Multiple BUS structure

D. BUS Programmer

E. None of these

Q.15 When the microcontroller executes some arithmetic operations, then the flag bits of which register are affected?

A. PSW   **B.** SP

C. DPTR   **D.** PC

E. None of these

Q.16 A proper conformal coating prevents PCB from______.

A. Corrosion

B. Humidity

C. Environmental Stress

D. Dust

E. All the above

Q.17 Which of the following is not an addressing mode of 8051?

A. Register instructions

B. Register specific instructions

C. Indexed addressing

D. (A) and (B) both

E. None of these

Q.18 If we push data onto the stack then the stack pointer-
A. Increases with every push
B. Decreases with every push
C. Increases & decreases with every push
D. No change
E. None of these

Q.19 A typical Solder composition used in component assembly to PCB is:

A. Lead and silver
B. Lead and copper
C. Lead and zinc
D. Lead and tin
E. None of these

Q.20 In microprocessors, the IC (instruction cycle), FC (fetch cycle) and EC (execution cycle) are related as

A. IC = FC - EC
B. IC = FC + EC
C. IC = FC + 2EC
D. EC = IC + FC
E. FC = IC + EC

Q.21 The manipulation of binary information is done by logic circuits called _________.

A. Blocks
B. Gates
C. Flip-Flops
D. Symbols
E. Keyboard

Q.22 1024 kilobytes are equal to-

A. 1 Megabyte
B. 1 Gigabyte
C. 10 Kilobyte
D. 1024 Bytes
E. None of these

Q.23 The pipelining process is also called as _____ .

A. Superscalar operation
B. Assembly line operation
C. Von Neumann cycle
D. Ultimate Operation
E. None of the mentioned

Q.24 Which of the following is not considered as a peripheral device?

A. CPU
B. Keyboard
C. Monitor
D. Joystick
E. Touchscreen

Q.25 A device that converts digital signals to analog signals is:

A. Modem
B. Packet
C. Keyboard
D. Both (B) and (C)
E. None of these

Q.26 The collection of 8-bits is called as -

A. Byte
B. Nibble
C. Word
D. Record
E. None of these

Q.27 What is the packaging technology used in integrated circuits to reduce space in PCB?

A. SMT
B. BBT
C. DIP
D. VLSI
E. SIVL

Q.28 The processor indicates to the devices that it is ready to receive interrupts ______.

A. By enabling the interrupt request line
B. By enabling the IRQ bits
C. By activating the interrupt acknowledge line
D. By Hyper Text Machine Link
E. None of these

Q.29 8051 microcontrollers are manufactured by which of the following companies?

A. Atmel
B. Philips
C. Intel
D. (A), (B) and (C)
E. None of these

Q.30 In computer MODEM stands for ______.

A. Modulator-Demodulator
B. Micro-Demonation
C. Micro-Demos
D. Mono-Demoe
E. None of these

// Smart Answer Sheet //

Correct Percentage of students who answered correctly. **Skipped** Percentage of students who skipped.

Q.	Ans.	Correct / Skipped	Q.	Ans.	Correct / Skipped	Q.	Ans.	Correct / Skipped	Q.	Ans.	Correct / Skipped	Q.	Ans.	Correct / Skipped	Q.	Ans.	Correct / Skipped	Q.	Ans.	Correct / Skipped
1	C	82.51 % / 16.08 %	6	B	61.12 % / 33.11 %	11	B	64.17 % / 30.64 %	16	E	56.6 % / 33.52 %	21	B	67.69 % / 31.96 %	26	A	40.58 % / 57.74 %			
2	B	83.64 % / 12.56 %	7	D	46.92 % / 39.91 %	12	C	80.78 % / 17.02 %	17	E	58.45 % / 32.58 %	22	A	81.29 % / 12.75 %	27	A	59.63 % / 40.13 %			
3	C	42.23 % / 50.58 %	8	C	60.74 % / 35.71 %	13	A	57.56 % / 31.12 %	18	A	82.06 % / 11.72 %	23	B	61.04 % / 37.12 %	28	C	43.96 % / 40.08 %			
4	C	68.43 % / 30.75 %	9	E	84.53 % / 11.35 %	14	B	76.9 % / 20.04 %	19	D	77.57 % / 16.97 %	24	A	48.7 % / 49.42 %	29	D	45.33 % / 49.66 %			
5	D	66.08 % / 33.71 %	10	B	48.61 % / 39.41 %	15	A	42.06 % / 34.4 %	20	B	17.61 % / 78.02 %	25	A	62.01 % / 35.17 %	30	A	86.98 % / 10.48 %			

//Hints and Solutions//

1. In 1945, Von-Neumann proposed his computer architecture design, and later it was known as the Von-Neumann Architecture. It consisted of a Control Unit, Arithmetic, and Logical Memory Unit (ALU), Registers, and Inputs/Outputs.

Hence, the correct option is (C).

2. A processor performing fetch or decoding of different instruction during the execution of another instruction is called Pipe-lining.

Pipe-lining is the process of improving the performance of the system by processing different instructions at the same time, with only one instruction performing one specific operation.

Hence, the correct option is (B).

3. The BUS busy activated indicates that the BUS is already allocated to a device and is being used.

A set of connected lines is also called a bus. Basically, a bus is a bundle of wires that are grouped together to serve a single purpose in the microprocessor, in which there are three set of communication lines that are called buses.

Hence, the correct option is (C).

4. A combinational circuit is a connected arrangement of logic gates with a set of inputs and outputs.

It consists of logic gates whose outputs at any instant of time are determined directly from the present combination of inputs without regard to previous input. Examples of combinational circuits: Adder, Subtractor, Converter, and Encoder/Decoder.

Hence, the correct option is (C).

5. Low-level languages are also known as Machine Language.

A low-level programming language is a programming language that provides little or no abstraction from a computer's instruction set architecture commands or functions in the language map closely to processor instructions.

Generally, this refers to either machine code or assembly language.

Hence, the correct option is (D).

6. The interrupt servicing mechanism in which the requesting device identifies itself to the processor to be serviced is vectored interrupts.

In a computer, a vectored interrupt is an I/O interrupt that tells the part of the computer that handles I/O interrupts at the hardware level that a request for attention from an I/O device has been received and also identifies the device that sent the request.

Hence, the correct option is (B).

7. The first leftmost bit i.e. the most significant bit (MSB) is used to represent the sign (+ve or -ve) for a given number. If the MSB is 1, the number is negative else if it is 0, the number is positive. Here, the +1=0001 and for -1=1001.

Hence, the correct option is (D).

8. The Code converter is used to convert one type of binary code to another. There are different types of binary codes like BCD code, gray code, excess-3 code, etc. To get the required code from any one type of code, the simple code conversion process is done with the help of combinational circuits.

Hence, the correct option is (C).

9. The CPU performs basic arithmetic, logic operation, arithmetic operation, logic, controlling, and input/output (I/O) operations specified by the instructions in the program. This contrasts with external components such as main memory and I/O circuitry, and specialized processors such as graphics processing units (GPUs).

Hence, the correct option is (E).

10. The IC chips for computers are generally made of silicon.

Integrated circuit (IC):

- It is also known as a microchip or a microelectronic circuit.

- The computers of the third generation used Integrated Circuits (ICs) in place of transistors.

- An IC is a collection of electronic components like resistors, transistors, capacitors, etc. all put together into a tiny chip to achieve a common goal. They are generally made of silicon. Silicon is used in electronic devices because it's a semiconductor.

Hence, the correct option is (B).

11. After the completion of the DMA transfer, the processor is notified by an Interrupt signal.

Once the current instruction execution is completed, the processor initiates the interrupt handling by saving the current register contents on the stack. The controller raises an interrupt signal to notify the processor that the transfer was complete.

Hence, the correct option is (B).

12. If any one of the input is 1, then the gate that gives 1 output, is known as OR gate.

An OR gate has two or more than two inputs and one output signal. It is called an OR gate because the output signal will be high only if any or all input signals are high.

Hence, the correct option is (C).

13. The 8051 contains two 16-bit registers: the program counter (PC) and the data pointer (DPTR). Each is used to hold the address of a byte in memory. The Data Pointer (DPTR) is the 8051's only user-accessible 16-bit (2-byte) register.

Hence, the correct option is (A).

14. To overcome the conflict over the possession of the BUS we use BUS arbitrators.

A conflict may arise if the number of DMA controllers or other controllers or processors try to access the common bus at the same time, but access can be given to only one of those. Only one processor or controller can be Bus master at the same point in time. To resolve these conflicts, the Bus Arbitration procedure is implemented to coordinate the activities of all devices requesting memory transfers. Bus Arbitration is performed by Bus Arbitrators.

Hence, the correct option is (B).

15. When the microcontroller executes some arithmetic operations, then the flag bits of PSW register are affected. PSW stands for program status word. It consists of carry, auxiliary carry, overflow, parity, register bank select bits etc. which are affected during such operations.

Hence, the correct option is (A).

16. Conformal coating is a protective non-conductive dielectric layer that is applied to the printed circuit board assembly to protect the electronic assembly from:

- Damage due to contamination
- Salt spray
- Moisture 'or' Humidity
- Dust and corrosion
- Harsh or extreme environmental stress.

The coating also prevents damage from rough handling, installation, reduction of mechanical and thermal stress.

It has a thickness of about 25 - 250 μm.

Hence, the correct option is (E).

17. Register instructions, register specific instructions and indexed addressing all are addressing mode of 8051. There are six addressing modes of 8051, i.e.

1. Direct addressing
2. Indirect addressing
3. Register instructions
4. Register specific(Register Implicit) instructions
5. Immediate mode
6. Indexed addressing.

Hence, the correct option is (E).

18. If we push elements onto the stack then the stack pointer increases with every push of the element. When a new data item is entered or "pushed" onto the top of a stack, the stack pointer increments to the next physical memory address, and the new item is copied to that address.

Hence, the correct option is (A).

19. On Printer Circuit Board the electronic devices are added or repaired used soldering of terminals to the board. The modern techniques involve using a solder gun.

In the Printed Circuit Board (PCB) the electronic components connected are Surface Mounted Devices, its pins are soldered onto the PCB using dip soldering method.

Soldering: Soldering is a joining process used to join different types of metals together having different properties. Solder is a metal alloy, usually made up of tin and lead which is melted using a hot iron (soldering iron).

Hence, the correct option is (D).

20. The Steps required by the CPU to fetch and execute an Instruction is called an instruction cycle. It consists of fetch and executes cycle.

Instruction cycle (IC) = Fetch cycle (FC) + Execution cycle (EC)

The time required by the microprocessor to complete the operation of accessing memory or I/O devices is called a machine cycle.

Clock time is a known time state. It is reciprocal of clock frequency.

Instruction cycle > Machine cycle > Clock cycle (time state).

Hence, the correct option is (B).

21. The manipulation of binary information is done by logic circuits called gates. Binary logic deals with binary variables and with operations that assume a logical meaning. It is used to describe, in algebraic or tabular form, the manipulation is done by logic circuits called gates.

Gates are blocks of hardware that produce graphic symbol and its operation can be described by means of an algebraic expression. The input-output relationship of the binary variables for each gate can be represented in tabular form by a truth-table.

Hence, the correct option is (B).

22. 1024 kilobytes are equal to 1 Megabytes.

Computer data storage conversions:

1 Kilobyte	1024 Bytes
1 Megabyte	1024 Kilobyte
1 Gigabyte	1024 Megabyte
1 Terabyte	1024 Gigabyte
1 Petabyte	1024 Terabyte

Hence, the correct option is (A).

23. The pipelining process is also called as Assembly line operation. Because it execute the operation line by line.,

Pipelining is the process of accumulating instruction from the processor through a pipeline. It allows storing and executing instructions in an orderly process and execution will be done one by one that's why it is called assembly line operation. A pipeline is divided into stages and these stages are connected with one another to form a pipe-like structure.

Hence, the correct option is (B).

24. The CPU is not considered as a peripheral device as it is the primary component of the computer, and a computer system cannot work without a CPU. Peripheral devices are not the essential parts of the computer and can be defined as an auxiliary device that connects to and works with the computer such as a mouse, keyboard, etc.

Hence, the correct option is (A).

25. Modem, (stands from "modulator/demodulator"), any of a class of electronic devices that convert digital data signals into modulated analog signals suitable for transmission over analog telecommunications circuits.

A modem also receives modulated signals and demodulates them, recovering the digital signal for use by the data equipment.

Modems thus make it possible for established telecommunications media to support a wide variety of data communication, such as e-mail between personal computers, facsimile transmission between fax machines, or the downloading of audio-video files from a World Wide Web server to a home computer.

Hence, the correct option is (A).

26. A Byte is a unit of data measurement which mainly consists of eight bits. A byte is a series of binary digits, which contain '0' or '1'. A byte is represented as upper-case 'B' whereas a bit is represented as small-case "b".

Hence, the correct option is (A).

27. Surface Mount Technology (SMT) is a method for constructing electronic circuits in which the components (SMC, or Surface Mounted Components) are mounted directly onto the surface of PCBs.

Electronic devices made for this purpose are called Surface-mount devices or SMD's.

Advantages of using Surface mount technology are:

- Lower power ratings
- Closer spacing of components along with the ability to use both sides of the PCB for component mounting. This results in efficient utilization of the Board surface.
- Better mechanical performance under shake and vibration conditions.

Hence, the correct option is (A).

28. The processor indicates to the devices that it is ready to receive interrupts by activating the interrupt acknowledge line.

When there is no interrupt the interrupt line stays in high level state. The CPU respond to the interrupt by enabling the interrupt acknowledge line. This signal is received by the device 1 at its PI input. The acknowledge signal passes to next device through PO output only if device 1 is not requesting an interrupt. When the processor activates the acknowledge line the devices send their interrupts to the processor.

Hence, the correct option is (C).

29. 8051 microcontrollers are manufactured by Intel, Atmel, Philips/Signetics, Infineon, Dallas Semi/Maxim. It is built with 40 pins DIP (dual inline package), 4kb of ROM storage and 128 bytes of RAM storage, 2 16-bit timers. It consists of are four parallel 8-bit ports, which are programmable as well as addressable as per the requirement.

Hence, the correct option is (D).

30. In computer, MODEM stands for Modulator-Demodulator.

- The modem is an electronic device that is used by a computer for sending and receiving information over telephone lines.

- Computer information is stored digitally, whereas information transmitted over telephone lines is transmitted in the form of analog waves.
- It converts analog signals into digital and vice-versa.
- It allows a computer, router, or switch to connect to access, connect internet.
- It takes the analog signal from a telephone line are cable wire and converts it in the form of the digital form (0s and 1s) and vice-versa.

Hence, the correct option is (A).

Q.1 Which language made up of binary coded instructions?
A. Machine
B. C
C. BASIC
D. High level
E. None of these

Q.2 A program that reads each of the instructions in mnemonic form and translates it into the machine-language equivalent is known as _________.
A. Machine language
B. Assembler
C. Interpreter
D. C program
E. Computer language

Q.3 Prolog comes under _________.
A. Logic Programming
B. Procedural Programming
C. OOP
D. Functional
E. None of the above

Q.4 A program that can execute high-level language programs, are known as ___________.
A. Compiler
B. Interpreter
C. Sensor
D. Circuitry
E. None of these

Q.5 What is required in each C program?
A. The program must have at least one function.
B. The program does not require any function.
C. Input data
D. Output data
E. None of these

Q.6 Which among the following is a high-level language used to develop software applications in compact, efficient code that can be run on different types of computers with minimal change?
A. FORTRAN
B. C
C. C++
D. ALGOL
E. COBOL

Q.7 What is a lint?
A. C compiler
B. Interactive debugger
C. Analyzing tool
D. C interpreter
E. None of these

Q.8 Source program is compiled to an intermediate form called __________.
A. Byte Code
B. Smart code
C. Executable code
D. Machine code
E. None of these

Q.9 ____________ is the assembly language for an imaginary architecture.
A. Byte code
B. Machine code
C. Native code
D. Executable code
E. Smart code

Q.10 JIT stands for?
A. Just in time
B. Jump in time
C. Jump in text
D. Jump in terms
E. None of these

Q.11 Which of the following features must be supported by any programming language to become a pure object-oriented programming language?
A. Encapsulation
B. Inheritance
C. Polymorphism
D. (A), (B) and (C)
E. None of these

Q.12 A function declared as the "friend" function can always access the data in ______.
A. The private part of its class
B. The part declared as public of its class
C. Class of which it is the member
D. (A) and (B) both
E. None of these

Q.13 Which of the following is the original creator of the C++ language?
A. Dennis Ritchie
B. Ken Thompson
C. Bjarne Stroustrup
D. Brian Kernighan
E. None of these

Q.14 Which of the following is not a part of the program division in COBOL?
A. Identification
B. Environment
C. Procedure
D. Compilation
E. Data

Q.15 A Borland Turbo Assembler is ________.
A. Nasm
B. Tasm
C. Gas
D. Asm
E. None of these

Q.16 What are the instructions that tell the assembler what to do?
A. Executable instructions
B. Pseudo-ops
C. Logical instructions
D. Macros
E. None of the above

Q.17 What kind of programming language is Java?
A. Object-oriented programming language
B. Relational programming language
C. Sixth-generation programming language
D. Database management programming language
E. None of these

Q.18 A language _______ is supported by MS .Net platform.
A. C **B.** C++ **C.** Java **D.** C#
E. C@

Q.19 Which of the following is not a characteristic of High-level languages?
A. Machine code
B. Platform independent
C. Interactive execution
D. User-friendly
E. None of these

Q.20 What programming language model is organized around "objects" rather than "actions"?
A. Java **B.** OOP **C.** Perl **D.** C++
E. C

Q.21 In FORTRAN, the declarations of variables can be modified using the _____ parameter.
A. kind **B.** make
C. select **D.** change
E. None of these

Q.22 Which is interpreted language?
A. C++ **B.** C
C. MATLAB **D.** FORTRAN
E. C#

Q.23 Which of the following option leads to the portability and security of Java?
A. Bytecode is executed by JVM
B. The applet makes the Java code secure and portable
C. Use of exception handling
D. Dynamic binding between objects
E. None of these

Q.24 Which was the first widely used high-level language developed in 1957?
A. C **B.** Java **C.** Fortran **D.** Cobol
E. C++

Q.25 A text file that contains our program is called as _________.
A. Exe file **B.** Doc file
C. Obj file **D.** Source file
E. None of these

Q.26 Which of the following is not a Java features?
A. Dynamic
B. Architecture Neutral
C. Use of pointers
D. Object-oriented
E. None of these

Q.27 _____ is used to find and fix bugs in Java programs.
A. JVM **B.** JRE
C. JDK **D.** JDB
E. None of these

Q.28 First statement in a fortran code is ________.
A. include statement **B.** import statement
C. program statement **D.** @data statement
E. None of these

Q.29 A Fortran is not _________ language.
A. System supported
B. Source supported
C. Case Sensitive
D. Programmer supported
E. Both (A) and (B)

Q.30 What does the expression float A=35/0 return?
A. 0 **B.** Not a Number
C. Infinity **D.** Run time exception
E. 1

// Smart Answer Sheet //

Correct Percentage of students who answered correctly. **Skipped** Percentage of students who skipped.

Q.	Ans.	Correct / Skipped	Q.	Ans.	Correct / Skipped	Q.	Ans.	Correct / Skipped	Q.	Ans.	Correct / Skipped	Q.	Ans.	Correct / Skipped	Q.	Ans.	Correct / Skipped
1	A	80.54 % / 15.03 %	6	E	64.65 % / 32.06 %	11	D	29.04 % / 67.66 %	16	A	46.68 % / 50.84 %	21	A	40.99 % / 30.69 %	26	C	88.91 % / 11.09 %
2	B	50.26 % / 45.07 %	7	C	67.15 % / 32.49 %	12	C	59.61 % / 31.86 %	17	A	84.71 % / 10.43 %	22	C	80.12 % / 17.57 %	27	D	85.47 % / 14.29 %
3	A	79.2 % / 14.33 %	8	A	41.41 % / 54.75 %	13	C	53.2 % / 34.93 %	18	D	85.1 % / 11.9 %	23	A	60.68 % / 33.88 %	28	C	40.83 % / 47.95 %
4	B	89.95 % / 10.04 %	9	A	42.33 % / 51.29 %	14	D	79.64 % / 17.5 %	19	A	83.79 % / 13.77 %	24	C	54.88 % / 39.55 %	29	C	86.16 % / 13.3 %
5	A	79.87 % / 16.75 %	10	A	76.04 % / 23.01 %	15	B	42.55 % / 43.74 %	20	B	48.44 % / 41.54 %	25	D	41.09 % / 34.27 %	30	C	81.84 % / 11.24 %

//Hints and Solutions//

1. The language made up of binary coded instructions built into the hardware of a particular computer and used directly by the computer is machine language. Machine language, or machine code, is a low-level language comprised of binary digits (ones and zeros). High-level languages, such as Swift and C++ must be compiled into machine language before the code is run on a computer.

Hence, the correct option is (A).

2. A program that reads each of the instructions in mnemonic form and translates it into the machine-language equivalent is known as Assembler. Assembler uses a mnemonic to represent each low-level machine instruction or opcode, typically also each architectural register, flag, etc.

Hence, the correct option is (B).

3. Prolog stands for Programming in Logic. Prolog differs from the most common programming languages because it is a declarative language. This means that the programmer must specify in detail how to solve a problem. Prolog is a type of logic programming. The options (A), (B), (C) and (D) mentioned are the four categories of programming.

Hence, the correct option is (A).

4. Interpreter is a program that can execute high-level language programs "directly," without first being translated into machine language. An Interpreter directly executes instructions written in a programming or scripting language without previously converting them to an object code or machine code. Examples of interpreted languages are Perl, Python and Matlab.

Hence, the correct option is (B).

5. Any C program has at least one function, and even the most trivial programs can specify additional functions. A function is a piece of code. In other words, it works like a sub-program.

Hence, the correct option is (A).

6. COBOL is a high-level language used to develop software applications in compact, efficient code that can be run on different types of computers with minimal change. It is compiled English-like computer programming language designed for business use. It object-oriented since 2002.

Hence, the correct option is (E).

7. Lint is an analyzing tool that analyzes the source code by suspicious constructions, stylistic errors, bugs, and flag programming errors. Lint is a compiler-like tool in which it parses the source files of C programming. It checks the syntactic accuracy of these files.

Hence, the correct option is (C).

8. The Source program is compiled to an intermediate form called byte code. For each supported platform, write a "virtual machine" emulator that reads byte code and emulates its execution.

Hence, the correct option is (A).

9. Byte code is the assembly language for an imaginary architecture. Bytecode is similar to assembly language in that it is not a high-level language, but it is still somewhat readable, unlike machine language. Both may be considered "intermediate languages" that fall between source code and machine code. The primary difference between the two is that bytecode is generated for a virtual machine (software), while assembly language is created for a CPU (hardware).

Hence, the correct option is (A).

10. JIT stands for Just in time. The JIT compiler aids in improving the performance of Java programs by compiling bytecode into native machine code at run time. The JIT compiler is enabled throughout, while it gets activated, when a method is invoked. For a compiled method, the JVM directly calls the compiled code, instead of interpreting it.

Hence, the correct option is (A).

11. There is nothing that forces a user to use the OOP concept in C++. In contrast, it is necessary for a programming language that it must support all three features as encapsulation, inheritance, and polymorphism completely to become a pure Object-Oriented Language.

Hence, the correct option is (D).

12. In C++, a member function can always access its class member variable, irrespective of the access specifier in which the member variable is declared. Therefore a member function can always access the data of the class of which it is a member.

Hence, the correct option is (C).

13. C++ is a general-purpose programming language created by Bjarne Stroustrup as an extension of the C programming language, or C with Classes. The language has expanded greatly over time, and modern C++ now has object-oriented, generic, and functional features in addition to features for low-level memory manipulation.

Hence, the correct option is (C).

14. Compilation is not a part of the program division in COBOL. COBOL has 4 basic parts in the division section: Identification, Environment, data and procedure. Each program is organized like a book.

Hence, the correct option is (D).

15. Tasm is the borland turbo assembler. Tasm is an assembler for software development published by Borland in 1989. It runs on and produces code for 16- or 32-bit x86 MS-DOS and compatibles or Microsoft Windows. It can be used with Borland's other language products: Turbo Pascal, Turbo Basic, Turbo C, and Turbo C++.

Hence, the correct option is (B).

16. The executable instructions or simple instructions tell the processor or assembler what to do. Each instruction consists of an operation code (opcode). Each executable instruction generates one machine language instruction.

Hence, the correct option is (A).

17. Java is an object-oriented, class-based, concurrent, secured and general-purpose computer-programming language. It is a widely used robust technology. Java is a programming language and a platform. Java was developed by Sun Microsystems in the year 1995. James Gosling is known as the father of Java.

Hence, the correct option is (A).

18. C# is a language supported by the MS. Net platform. C# is a general-purpose, multi-paradigm programming language encompassing static typing, strong typing, lexically scoped, imperative, declarative, functional, generic, object-oriented (class-based), and component-oriented programming disciplines.

Programming Languages which are designed and developed by Microsoft are:

- C#.NET
- VB.NET
- C++.NET
- J#.NET
- F#.NET
- JSCRIPT.NET
- WINDOWS POWERSHELL
- IRON RUBY
- IRON PYTHON
- C OMEGA
- ASML(Abstract State Machine Language)

Hence, the correct option is (D).

19. Machine code is not a characteristic of High-level languages. High-level languages are not in machine language. It is converted to machine language for further processing. A high-level language (HLL) is a programming language such as C, Fortan, or Pascal that enables a programmer to write programs that are more or less independent of a particular type of computer. Such languages are considered high-level because they are closer to human languages and further from machine languages.

Hence, the correct option is (A).

20. OOP programming language model is organized around "objects" rather than "actions". Object-oriented programming is based on the concept of objects. In object-oriented programming data structures, or objects are defined, each with its own properties or attributes. Each object can also contain its own procedures or methods. Software is designed by using objects that interact with one another.

Hence, the correct option is (B).

21. In FORTRAN, the declarations of variables can be modified using the kind parameter. It can often be used for the precision of reals. If you want to change the precision, it can easily be done using one line of code.

Hence, the correct option is (A).

22. MATLAB is an interpreted language. All the other languages are compiled languages. In the case of Interpreted language, the translation to machine-language is performed incrementally at run-time. MATLAB is a proprietary multi-paradigm programming language and numeric computing environment developed by MathWorks. MATLAB allows matrix manipulations, plotting of functions and data, implementation of algorithms, creation of user interfaces, and interfacing with programs written in other languages.

Hence, the correct option is (C).

23. The output of the Java compiler is bytecode, which leads to the security and portability of the Java code. It is a highly developed set of instructions that are designed to be executed by the Java runtime system known as Java Virtual Machine (JVM). The Java programs executed by the JVM that makes the code portable and secure. Because JVM prevents the code from generating its side effects. The Java code is portable, as the same byte code can run on any platform.

Hence, the correct option is (A).

24. Fortran which stands for Formula Translation was the first widely-used high level language, which was developed in 1957. It was developed by IBM for scientific applications. The program was entered as punch cards.

Hence, the correct option is (C).

25. A text file that contains our program is called as source file. A source file is a glorified text file with program instructions written in a specific programming language like, C or Java or Python. You can compile or interpret this file to run the program. When the source file has been compiled it's basically transformed/translated into a lower level language like Assembly.

Hence, the correct option is (D).

26. The Java language does not support pointers; some of the major reasons are listed below:

- One of the major factors of not using pointers in Java is security concerns. Due to pointers, most of the users consider C-language very confusing and complex. This is the reason why Green Team (Java Team members) has not introduced pointers in Java.

- Java provides an effective layer of abstraction to the developers by not using pointers in Java.

Java is dynamic, architecture-neutral, and object-oriented programming language.

Hence, the correct option is (C).

27. The Java Debugger (JDB or jdb) is a command-line java debugger that debugs the java class. It is a part of the Java Platform Debugger Architecture (JPDA) that helps in the inspections and debugging of a local or remote Java Virtual Machine (JVM).

The JVM (Java Virtual Machine) enables a computer to run Java or other language (kotlin, groovy, Scala, etc.) programs that are compiled to the Java bytecode. The JRE (Java Runtime Environment) is a part of JDK that contains the Java class libraries, Java class loader, and the Java Virtual Machine. The JDK (Java Development Kit) is a software development environment used to develop Java applications and applets.

Hence, the correct option is (D).

28. First statement in a fortran code is program statement. The first statement of this program begins with the word program. It is a non-executable statement that specifies the name of the program to the Fortran compiler. Its name can be up to 31 characters long and can be any combination of alphabetic characters, digits, and underscores.

Hence, the correct option is (C).

29. Fortran is not a case sensitive language. For e.g. Program xyz also works. Also multiple consecutive blank spaces are ignored. Fortran is a general-purpose, compiled imperative programming language that is especially suited to numeric computation and scientific computing. It is a popular language for high-performance computing and is used for programs that benchmark and rank the world's fastest supercomputers.

Hence, the correct option is (C).

30. In Java, whenever we divide any number (double, float, and long except integer) by zero, it results in infinity. According to the IEEE Standard for Floating-Point Arithmetic (IEEE 754), if we divide 1/0 will give positive infinity, -1/0 will give negative infinity, and 0/0 will give NaN. But on dividing an integer by zero, it throws a runtime exception, i.e., java.lang.ArithmeticException.

Hence, the correct option is (C).

Q.1 Which of the following terms is just the connection of networks that can be joined together?

A. Internet
B. Virtual private network
C. Intranet
D. Extranet
E. None of these

Q.2 A computer checks the _____ of user names and passwords for a match before granting access.

A. Website
B. Network
C. Backup file
D. Database
E. None of these

Q.3 Network components are connected to the same cable in the _____ topology.

A. Star
B. Ring
C. Bus
D. Mesh
E. None of these

Q.4 What is backup?

A. Adding more components to your network
B. Protecting data by copying it from the original source to a different destination
C. Filtering old data from the new data
D. (A) and (B) both
E. All of the above

Q.5 WPA2 is used for security in ________.

A. Internet
B. Bluetooth
C. Wi-Fi
D. (A) and (B) both
E. All of the above

Q.6 Complex networks today are made up of hundreds and sometimes thousands of ________.

A. Documents
B. Components
C. Servers
D. Entities
E. None of these

Q.7 The first Network is ________.

A. CNNET
B. NSFNET
C. ASAPNET
D. ARPANET
E. None of these

Q.8 A USB communication device that supports data encryption for secure wireless communication for notebook users is called a _____.

A. USB wireless network adapter
B. Wireless switch
C. Wireless hub
D. Router
E. All of the above

Q.9 Which of the following is the most common shared resource in a computer network?

A. Keyboard
B. Mouse
C. Combo drive
D. Printer
E. None of these

Q.10 What is Web Casting?

A. Casting a Mobile TV Star in a role on the web
B. Transmitting the video and audio on the Internet
C. Playing of Music on the Internet
D. Searching on the Web
E. All of the above

Q.11 Which NetWare protocol works on layer 3–network layer—of the OSI model?

A. IPX
B. NCP
C. SPX
D. NetBIOS
E. All of the above

Q.12 What is the full form of ISP?

A. Interface Segregation Principle
B. Internet Segregation Principle
C. Informal Segregation Principle
D. (A) and (B) both
E. All of the above

Q.13 In which method we can connect to internet?

A. Dial-up
B. SLIP
C. PPP
D. (A) and (B) both
E. All of these

Q.14 The three types of IP addresses are:

A. Network Address, Host Address, Local Address
B. Network Address, Host Address, Broad Cast Address
C. Network Address, Host Address, Packet Address
D. Network Address, Host Address, Frame Address
E. None of these

Q.15 A network that needs human beings to manually route signals is called:

A. Fiber Optic Network
B. Bus Network
C. T-switched network
D. Ring network
E. None of these

Q.16 DNS can obtain the ________ of host if its domain name is known and vice versa.

A. Station address
B. IP address
C. Port address
D. Checksum
E. None of these

Q.17 A network, which is used for sharing data, software and hardware among several users of microcomputers, is called-

A. Wide Area Network.
B. Metropolitan Area Network.
C. Local Area Network.

D.   Value Added Network.
E.   All of the above

Q.18 A VLAN equals to ________.
A. Router
B. Subnet
C. Firewall
D. Host/Client ID
E. None of these

Q.19 An example of a medium speed, switched communications service is
A. Series 1000
B. Data phone 50
C. DDD
D. (A) and (B) both
E. None of these

Q.20 Wide area networks (WANs) always require
A.   High bandwidth communication source link
B.   High speed processors
C.   Same type
D.   (A) and (B) both
E.   None of the above

Q.21 The Sharing of a medium and its path by two or more devices is called-
A. Modulation
B. Encoding
C. Multiplexing
D. Line discipline
E. None of these

Q.22 Which of the following statements is true?
A.   TCP / IP Model developed before OSI model.
B.   TCP / IP model developed after the OSI model
C.   TCP / IP model developed simaltaneousaly to the Model OSI model
D.   TCP / IP model developed to overcome the shortcomings of OSI Model.
E.   None of these

Q.23 What is the use of FTP?
A.   To view a file on a remote computer
B.   To identify the name of the domain
C.   To identify the name of the host
D.   To send the file to the network
E.   None of these

Q.24 Which of the following wire-network remains within an office?
A. LAN
B. WAN
C. cellular network
D. MAN
E. None of these

Q.25 How many TCP connections does FTP use?
A. one
B. two
C. three
D. four
E. None of these

Q.26 What do we call a network whose elements may be separated by some distance, it usually involves two or more small networks and dedicated high speed telephone lines?
A. URL   **B.** LAN   **C.** WAN   **D.** WWW
E. MAN

Q.27 What is the maximum data capacity for optical fiber cable?
A. 10 mbps
B. 100 mbps
C. 1000 mbps
D. 10000 mbps
E. None of these

Q.28 If a computer on the network shares, resources for other to use, it is called ________.
A. Server
B. Client
C. Mainframe
D. (A) and (B) both
E. All of the above

Q.29 What is work of TDM?
A.   Several signals are sent in a time slotted mode on a channel
B.   Several signals are sent on separate channels at a time
C.   One signal is sent to several users
D.   (A) and (B) both
E.   All of the above

Q.30 MODEM word is made from:
A.   Modulation, Demodulation
B.   Modulation, Rough modulation
C.   Modulation, Defination
D.   (A) and (B) both
E.   All of above

// Smart Answer Sheet //

Correct Percentage of students who answered correctly. **Skipped** Percentage of students who skipped.

Q.	Ans.	Correct / Skipped	Q.	Ans.	Correct / Skipped	Q.	Ans.	Correct / Skipped	Q.	Ans.	Correct / Skipped	Q.	Ans.	Correct / Skipped	Q.	Ans.	Correct / Skipped
1	A	66.36 % / 31.31 %	6	B	61.17 % / 36.33 %	11	A	24.86 % / 68.26 %	16	B	64.97 % / 31.95 %	21	C	59.06 % / 37.62 %	26	C	66.77 % / 31.79 %
2	D	64.84 % / 31.39 %	7	D	64.22 % / 32.71 %	12	A	12.96 % / 69.12 %	17	C	69.24 % / 30.54 %	22	A	67.28 % / 31.95 %	27	C	55.43 % / 36.48 %
3	C	81.54 % / 12.24 %	8	A	40.48 % / 31.87 %	13	E	22.49 % / 73.23 %	18	B	43.43 % / 39.81 %	23	D	46.83 % / 37.88 %	28	A	60.55 % / 34.19 %
4	B	79.55 % / 12.51 %	9	D	65.07 % / 33.68 %	14	B	24.94 % / 69.53 %	19	C	60.34 % / 33.05 %	24	A	50.09 % / 39.99 %	29	A	41.5 % / 36.2 %
5	C	58.95 % / 32.31 %	10	B	28.26 % / 67.5 %	15	C	40.79 % / 47.01 %	20	E	53.04 % / 42.69 %	25	B	66.07 % / 30.36 %	30	A	54.46 % / 31.96 %

//Hints and Solutions//

1. The internet is a globally connected network system that uses TCP/IP to transmit data via various types of media. The internet is a network of global exchanges – including private, public, business, academic and government networks – connected by guided, wireless and fiber-optic technologies.

Hence, the correct option is (A).

2. A database is an organized collection of data, generally stored and accessed electronically from a computer system. Where databases are more complex they are often developed using formal design and modeling techniques

Hence, the correct option is (D).

3. A bus topology is a topology for a Local Area Network (LAN) in which all the nodes are connected to a single cable. The cable to which the nodes connect is called a "backbone". If the backbone is broken, the entire segment fails.

Hence, the correct option is (C).

4. In information technology, a backup, or data backup, or the process of backing up, refers to the copying into an archive file of computer data so it may be used to restore the original after a data loss event.

Hence, the correct option is (B).

5. WPA2 is a type of encryption used to secure the vast majority of Wi-Fi networks. A WPA2 network provides unique encryption keys for each wireless client that connects to it.

Hence, the correct option is (C).

6. Complex networks today are made up of hundreds and sometimes thousands of components. For the effective functioning of these thousands of components, good network management is essential.

Hence, the correct option is (B).

7. The Advanced Research Projects Agency Network (ARPANET) was an early packet-switching network and the first network to implement the protocol suite TCP/IP. Both technologies became the technical foundation of the Internet.

Hence, the correct option is (D).

8. USB wireless network adapter is a communication device that plugs into a USB port and usually provides an intuitive graphical user interface (GUI) for easy configuration. It supports data encryption for secure wireless communication and is perfect for the traveler and notebook user.

Hence, the correct option is (A).

9. Printer is the most common shared resource in a computer network. A combo drive is a type of optical drive that combines CD-R/CD-RW recording capability with an ability to read (but not write) DVD media; some manufacturers refer this as CD-RW/DVD-ROM drive.

Hence, the correct option is (D).

10. Web Casting is Transmitting the video and audio on the Internet. Webcasting is the process of video broadcasting live over the internet. This technology operates in real-time and allows for active conversations among and between the webcaster and their viewers.

Hence, the correct option is (B).

11. IPX (Internetwork Packet Exchange) is the NetWare network layer 3 protocol used for transferring information on LANs that use Novell's NetWare.

Hence, the correct option is (A).

12. The interface-segregation principle states that no client should be forced to depend on methods it does not use. ISP splits interfaces that are very large into smaller and more specific ones so that clients will only have to know about the methods that are of interest to them.

Hence, the correct option is (A).

13. Dial-up Internet access is a form of Internet access that uses the facilities of the public switched telephone network to establish a connection to an Internet service provider by dialing a telephone number on a conventional telephone line.SLIP (Serial Line Internet Protocol) is the result of the integration of modem protocols prior to the suite of TCP/IP protocols. Point-to-Point Protocol (PPP) is a data link layer communications protocol used to establish a direct connection between two nodes.

Hence, the correct option is (E).

14. Host address is the portion of the address used to identify hosts and network address is an identifier for a node or network interface of a telecommunications network. The broadcast address represents all devices of the network. If an IP packet is sent on a broadcast address, it is intended for all devices of that network.

Hence, the correct option is (B).

15. A network that needs human beings to manually route signals is called a T-switched network. A network switch (also called switching hub, bridging hub, officially MAC bridge) is a computer networking device.

Hence, the correct option is (C).

16. DNS can obtain the IP address of the host if its domain name is known and vice versa. DNS automatically converts between the names we type in our Web browser address bar to the IP addresses of Web servers hosting.

Hence, the correct option is (B).

17. A local area network is a group of computers and associated devices that share a common communications line or wireless link to a server. A local area network is a computer network that interconnects computers within a limited area such as a residence, school, laboratory, university campus or office building.

Hence, the correct option is (C).

18. VLAN and Subnet are both developed to deal with segmenting or partitioning a portion of the network. And they also share such similarities as restricting broadcast domains or ensuring security through isolation of different sub-networks.

Hence, the correct option is (B).

19. The domain-driven design (DDD) approach enables the development of software that is focused on the complex requirements of those that need it and doesn't waste effort on anything unneeded. The clients of domain-driven design are often enterprise-level businesses.

Hence, the correct option is (C).

20. A WAN is a communications network that spans a large geographic area such as across cities, states, or countries. They can be private to connect parts of a business or they can be more public to connect smaller networks together.

Hence, the correct option is (E).

21. Multiplexing is a method by which multiple analog or digital signals are combined into one signal over a shared medium. The multiplexed signal is transmitted over a communication channel such as a cable. Multiplexing divides the capacity of the communication channel into several logical changes.

Hence, the correct option is (C).

22. The TCP/IP model, which is realistically the Internet Model, came into existence about 10 years before the OSI model. The four-layer Internet model defines the Internet protocol suite, better known as the TCP/IP suite.

Hence, the correct option is (A).

23. FTP is used to transfer files between computers on a network. You can use FTP to exchange files between computer accounts, transfer files between an account and a desktop computer, or access online software archives.

Hence, the correct option is (D).

24. Local Area Network (LAN) might connect together devices over a distance measured in tens of metres. At work or school, the LAN might connect devices over hundreds of metres. A Wide Area Network operates over a much larger area, as they interconnect LANs to allow them to exchange data

Hence, the correct option is (A).

25. FTP uses two TCP connections for communication. One to pass control information, and is not used to send files on port 21, only control information. And the other, a data connection on port 20 to send the data files between the client and the server.

Hence, the correct option is (B).

26. WAN networks may be separated by some distance, it usually involves two or more small networks and dedicated high speed telephone lines.TCP/IP is used for a WAN in combination with devices such as routers, switches, firewalls and modems.

Hence, the correct option is (C).

27. 1000 Enabled Capabilities Enabled to be enabled in particular applicable conditions, when enabled to charge, is changed as being capable of communication with the camera.

Hence, the correct option is (C).

28. Server gives the permission to sharing the resources of the computer in the network that is used by the client which is connected to that server. The client gives the request to the server for the services according to her request the server response and shared the resources and providing the services to the client in the network. The processor of the server is more powerful as compare to the client computer because it handles lots of requests. If the server is crash then nothing can be done.

Hence, the correct option is (A).

29. Time-division multiplexing (TDM) is a method of transmitting and receiving independent signals over a common signal path by means of synchronized switches at each end of the transmission line so that each signal appears on the line, only a fraction of time in an alternating pattern.

Hence, the correct option is (A).

30. Modem is short for "Modulator / Demodulator" that allows a computer or other device, such as a router or switch, to connect to the Internet. It converts or "modulates" an analog signal from a telephone or cable wire to a digital signal that a computer can recognize. Similarly, it converts outgoing digital data from a computer or other device to an analog signal.

Hence, the correct option is (A).

Q.1 Any electronic holding place where data can be stored and retrieved later whenever required is __________?
A. memory
B. drive
C. disk
D. circuit
E. None of these

Q.2 Which of the following is the fastest means of memory access for CPU?
A. Registers
B. Cache
C. Main memory
D. Virtual Memory
E. None of the above

Q.3 The memory implemented using the semiconductor chips is _______.
A. Cache
B. Main
C. Secondary
D. Registers
E. None of these

Q.4 Size of the ______ memory mainly depends on the size of the address bus.
A. Main
B. Virtual
C. Secondary
D. Cache
E. None of these

Q.5 Which of the following is independent of the address bus?
A. Secondary memory
B. Main memory
C. Onboard memory
D. Cache memory
E. primary memory

Q.6 __________ storage is a system where a robotic arm will connect or disconnect off-line mass storage media according to the computer operating system demands.
A. Secondary
B. Virtual
C. Tertiary
D. Magnetic
E. Primary

Q.7 What is the location of the internal registers of CPU?
A. Internal
B. On-chip
C. External
D. Motherboard
E. None of these

Q.8 MAR stands for __________.
A. Memory address register
B. Main address register
C. Main accessible register
D. Memory accessible register
E. None of the above

Q.9 Storage which stores or retains data after power off is called-
A. Volatile storage
B. Non- volatile storage
C. Sequential storage
D. Direct storage
E. None of the above

Q.10 The computer has a built-in system clock that emits millions of regularly spaced electric pulses per ____ called clock cycles.
A. second
B. millisecond
C. microsecond
D. minute
E. None of these

Q.11 The operation that does not involves clock cycles is __________.
A. Installation of a device
B. Execute
C. Fetch
D. Decode
E. None of these

Q.12 The number of clock cycles per second is referred to as _____.
A. Clock speed
B. Clock frequency
C. Clock rate
D. Clock timing
E. None of these

Q.13 CISC stands for __________.
A. Complex Information Sensed CPU
B. Complex Instruction Set Computer
C. Complex Intelligence Sensed CPU
D. Complex Instruction Set CPU
E. None of these

Q.14 Which of the following processor has a fixed length of instructions?
A. CISC
B. RISC
C. EPIC
D. Multi-core
E. None of the above

Q.15 Processor which is complex and expensive to produce ________.
A. RISC
B. EPIC
C. CISC
D. multi-core
E. None of these

Q.16 The architecture uses a tighter coupling between the compiler and the processor.
A. EPIC
B. Multi-core
C. RISC
D. CISC
E. All of these

Q.17 HLDA stands for ______.
A. High-level data
B. High-level data acknowledgment
C. Hold Acknowledgement
D. Hold Data
E. None of these

Q.18 Word length of a personal computer __________.

A. 64 bits   **B.** 16 bits
C. 8 bits   **D.** 32 bits
E. 1024 bytes

Q.19 _____________ is also called auxiliary storage.
A. Secondary memory   **B.** Tertiary memory
C. Primary memory   **D.** Cache memory
E. Both (A) and (B)

Q.20 Magnetic tape is a type of _______ access device.
A. Sequential   **B.** Direct access
C. Step   **D.** Indirect
E. None of these

Q.21 The magnetic tape is generally a plastic ribbon coated with _____.
A. Magnesium oxide   **B.** Chromium dioxide
C. Zinc oxide   **D.** Copper oxide
E. Both (A) and (B)

Q.22 The dots on the magnetic tape represent _______.
A. Binary digits   **B.** Decimal digits
C. Hex digits   **D.** Oct digits
E. None of these

Q.23 Which of the following is the correct representation for a storage capacity of a tape?
A. Data recording density = Storage capacity
B. Length = Storage capacity
C. Storage capacity= Length × data recording density
D. Storage capacity= Length + data recording density
E. None of the above

Q.24 _______________ is the amount of data that can be stored on a given length of tape.
A. Storage capacity
B. Length
C. Data recording density
D. Tape density
E. All of the above

Q.25 The number of characters/second that can be transmitted to the memory from the tape is denoted by the term.
A. Data transfer rate   **B.** Transmission mode
C. Transmission rate   **D.** Data mode
E. None of the above

Q.26 The typical value of data transfer rate is _________.
A. 7.7 MB/s   **B.** 6.6 MB/s
C. 5.5 MB/s   **D.** 10 MB/s
E. 15 MB/s

Q.27 Tape drive is connected to and controlled by _______.
A. Interpreter   **B.** Tape controller
C. CPU   **D.** Processor
E. Monitor

Q.28 _____________ is used for writing/reading of data to/from a magnetic ribbon.
A. Magnetic disk   **B.** Magnetic tape

C. Magnetic frames   **D.** Magnetic Ribbon
E. None of these

Q.29 The disk's surface is divided into a number of invisible concentric circles called:
A. Drives   **B.** Tracks
C. Slits   **D.** References
E. None of the above

Q.30 The number of sectors per track on a magnetic disk _______.
A. less than 5   **B.** 10 or more
C. 8 or more   **D.** less than 7
E. None of these

// Smart Answer Sheet //

| Correct | Percentage of students who answered correctly. | Skipped | Percentage of students who skipped. |

Q.	Ans.	Correct / Skipped	Q.	Ans.	Correct / Skipped	Q.	Ans.	Correct / Skipped	Q.	Ans.	Correct / Skipped	Q.	Ans.	Correct / Skipped	Q.	Ans.	Correct / Skipped
1	A	62.78 % / 30.37 %	6	C	60.63 % / 31.29 %	11	A	64.1 % / 30.2 %	16	A	45.47 % / 34.27 %	21	B	57.67 % / 31.96 %	26	A	47.57 % / 46.42 %
2	A	48.07 % / 46.89 %	7	B	50.1 % / 31.08 %	12	A	49.98 % / 43.18 %	17	C	47.85 % / 30.47 %	22	A	45.46 % / 41.31 %	27	B	58.7 % / 41.17 %
3	B	59.3 % / 34.47 %	8	A	64.62 % / 34.48 %	13	B	62.04 % / 34.94 %	18	C	41.29 % / 37.71 %	23	C	63.29 % / 35.44 %	28	B	58.0 % / 41.28 %
4	A	69.39 % / 30.01 %	9	B	65.3 % / 31.11 %	14	B	50.36 % / 42.19 %	19	A	62.75 % / 35.99 %	24	C	54.79 % / 40.06 %	29	B	58.28 % / 38.37 %
5	A	56.29 % / 30.34 %	10	A	61.3 % / 34.19 %	15	C	50.14 % / 42.77 %	20	A	41.1 % / 43.13 %	25	A	62.24 % / 32.22 %	30	C	56.98 % / 33.37 %

//Hints and Solutions//

1. Memory is the place where data can be stored and later retrieved. Memory can be of classified into register, cache, main memory, etc.

Hence, the correct option is (A).

2. Registers are the fastest means of access for CPU. Registers are the small memory locations which are present closest to the CPU.

Hence, the correct option is (A).

3. The main memory is implemented using semiconductor chips. The main memory is located on the motherboard. It mainly consists of RAM and a small amount of ROM.

Hence, the correct option is (B).

4. The size of the main memory depends on the size of the address bus of the CPU. The main memory mainly consists of RAM and ROM, where RAM contains the current data and programs and ROM contains permanent programs like BIOS.

Hence, the correct option is (A).

5. The secondary memory is independent of the address bus. It increases the storage space. It is implemented in the form of magnetic storage devices. Examples of this are hard disks and solid-state drives etc.

Hence, the correct option is (A).

6. Tertiary storage is a system where offline mass storage media is connected or disconnected according to the demand of a robotic arm computer operating system. It is used in the realms of enterprise storage and scientific computing on large computer systems and business computer networks and is something a typical personal computer never sees firsthand.

Hence, the correct option is (C).

7. The internal registers are present on-chip. They are therefore present inside the CPU. L1 cache is also present on-chip inside the CPU. Chip is an integrated circuit or small wafer of semiconductor material embedded with integrated circuitry.

Hence, the correct option is (B).

8. The MAR stands for memory address register. It holds the address of the active memory location. the memory address register (MAR) is the CPU register that either stores the memory address from which data will be fetched to the CPU or the address to which data will be sent and stored.

Hence, the correct option is (A).

9. Non-volatile memory (NVM) is a type of computer memory that has the capability to hold saved data even if the power is turned off. Non-volatile memory is highly popular among digital media; it is widely used in memory chips for USB memory sticks and digital cameras. Non-volatile memory eradicates the need for relatively slow types of secondary storage systems, including hard disks.

Hence, the correct option is (B).

10. The computer has a built-in system clock that emits millions of regularly spaced electric pulses per second called clock cycles. The regularly spaced electric pulses per second are referred to as clock cycles. All the jobs performed by the processor are on the basis of clock cycles.

Hence, the correct option is (A).

11. Normally, several clock cycles are required to fetch, execute and decode a particular program. Installation of a device is done by the system on its own. There is no need clock cycle.

Hence, the correct option is (A).

12. The number of clock cycles per second is the clock speed. It is generally measured in gigahertz(109 cycles/sec) or megahertz (106 cycles/sec).

Hence, the correct option is (A).

13. CISC stands for "Complex Instruction Set Computer". CISC is a large instruction set computer. It has variable-length instructions. It also has a variety of addressing modes.

Hence, the correct option is (B).

14. The RISC which stands for Reduced Instruction set computer has a fixed length of instructions. It has a small instruction set. Also has reduced references to memory to retrieve operands.

Hence, the correct option is (B).

15. CISC stands for complex instruction set computer. It is mostly used in personal computers. It has a large instruction set and a variable length of instructions.

Hence, the correct option is (C).

16. EPIC stands for Explicitly parallel instruction computing. It has a tighter coupling between the compiler and the processor. It enables the compiler to extract maximum parallelism in the original code.

Hence, the correct option is (A).

17. The full name of HLDA is "Hold Acknowledgment". The HOLD signal is given to the CPU whenever an interrupt is to be served. If the CPU is ready to give control of the bus, it gives the HLDA command which is Hold Acknowledgement.

Hence, the correct option is (C).

18. The word length which is the size of a word is generally 8 bits in a personal computer. Word Size is generally the number of bits that can be processed in one go by the CPU.

Hence, the correct option is (C).

19. The secondary memory which allows us to store a large amount of data is often referred to as the auxiliary memory. It generally stores a large amount of data on a permanent basis.

Hence, the correct option is (A).

20. Magnetic tapes are sequential access devices. They are secondary storage devices and are used to store large amounts of data. In sequential access, data can be retrieved in the same sequence in which it is stored.

Hence, the correct option is (A).

21. The plastic ribbon is coated with a magnetizable recording material. Iron oxide and chromium dioxide are generally used in magnetic tapes. Data are recorded on the tape in the form of tiny invisible dots.

Hence, the correct option is (B).

22. The data recorded on the tape in in the form of tiny invisible magnetized and non-magnetized spots (representing 1s and 0s) on its coated surface.

Hence, the correct option is (A).

23. Storage capacity is nothing but the product of length and data recording density. Magnetic tape is a commonly used sequential-access secondary device. Data recording density is measured in bytes per inch.

Hence, the correct option is (C).

24. Data recording density is the amount of data that can be stored on a given length of the tape. It is measured in bytes per inch. Bytes per inch=bpi.

Hence, the correct option is (C).

25. The transfer rate measurement unit is bytes/second(bps). Value depends on the data recording density and the speed with which the tape travels under the read/write head.

Hence, the correct option is (A).

26. Data transfer rate is defined as the number of characters per second that can be transmitted to the memory from tape. The typical value is 7.7 megabytes per second.

Hence, the correct option is (A).

27. The tape drive is connected to and controlled by a tape controller that interprets the commands for operating the tape drive. Certain commonly used commands are read, write, erase tape, etc.

Hence, the correct option is (B).

28. The magnetic tape ribbon is used for the same. It has read/write heads for reading/writing of data on the tape. When processing is complete, the tape is removed from the tape drive for offline storage.

Hence, the correct option is (B).

29. The concentric circles are called tracks. The tracks are numbered consecutively from outermost to innermost starting from zero. The number of tracks on a disk may be as few as 40 on small-capacity disks to several thousand on large capacity disks.

Hence, the correct option is (B).

30. Each track of a disk is subdivided into sectors. There are 8 or more sectors per track. Disk drives are designed to read/write only whole sectors at a time.

Hence, the correct option is (C).

Q.1 Identify the DBMS among the following.

A. PL/SQL **B.** MS – PowerPoint
C. MS – Access **D.** MS- Excel
E. None of these

Q.2 What package of MS Office 2007 manages RDBMS?

A. Excel **B.** Access
C. Goove **D.** OneNote
E. None of these

Q.3 Which of the following do not use a DBMS?

A. Ultimate users
B. Administrators
C. Database Designers
D. Hardware support teams
E. None of these

Q.4 What is the difference between DBMS and RDBMS?

A. A DBMS can be manipulated but an RDBMS cannot be
B. A DBMS is a database of commercial type by an RDBMS is a data of engineers
C. A DBMS cannot link up various files with one another whereas an RDBMS can
D. Both (A) and (B)
E. None of these

Q.5 In DBMS, a defined field can have __________.

A. A fixed length
B. An unlimited length
C. A fixed-length defined by data type
D. An unlimited length defined by programmer
E. None of these

Q.6 Which one of the following is an RDBMS?

A. Java Beans **B.** Fox Pro
C. Oracle **D.** DBase IV
E. All of the above

Q.7 Entities having a primary key are called?

A. Primary Entities **B.** Strong Entities
C. Weak Entities **D.** Primary Key
E. All of the above

Q.8 A transparent DBMS __________.

A. Cannot hide sensitive information from users
B. Keep its logical structure hidden from users
C. Keeps its physical structure hidden from users
D. (A) and (B) both
E. None of these

Q.9 The data stored in a database must be independent of the applications that access the database. This rule is called __________.

A. Logical Data Independence
B. Physical Data Independence
C. Data Dependency
D. (A) and (B) both
E. None of these

Q.10 Name the data in a database that must be independent of its user's view and any change in logical data must not affect the applications using it.

A. Logical Data Independence
B. Physical Data Independence
C. Data Redundancy
D. Data Logic
E. None of these

Q.11 Name the system in which the end-user must not be able to see that the data is distributed over various locations.

A. Distribution Independence
B. Distribution Dependence
C. Logic Dependence
D. Distribution Logic
E. None of these

Q.12 Name the database that must be independent of the application that uses it.

A. Integrity Rule
B. Logical Rule
C. Logical Relationship
D. Integrity Independence
E. None of these

Q.13 Related fields in a database are grouped to form a __________.

A. Data File **B.** Data Record
C. Menu **D.** Bank
E. None of these

Q.14 Consider the attributes ID, CITY and NAME. Which one of these can be considered as a super key?

A. NAME **B.** ID
C. CITY **D.** CITY , ID
E. None of these

Q.15 The purpose of the primary key in a database is to __________.

A. Unlock the database
B. Provide a map of the data
C. Uniquely identify a record
D. Establish constraints on database operations
E. All of the above

Q.16 Name the database object in MS Access that stores a question about the data in the database?

A. Table **B.** Form
C. Query **D.** Report
E. None of these

Q.17 What will be the normal form of a table after normalization in which all determinants are candidate key?

A. BCNF   **B.** 2NF
C. 5NF   **D.** 4NF
E. All of the above

Q.18 An expression builder is an access tool that controls an expression _________ for entering an expression.

A. Table   **B.** Box
C. Cell   **D.** Palette
E. None of these

Q.19 DML language is used to _________.

A. Define schema
B. Define internal level
C. Access Data
D. (A) and (B) both
E. None of these

Q.20 The view of total database content is _________.

A. Conceptual view   **B.** Internal view
C. External view   **D.** Physical View
E. None of these

Q.21 Which of the following is the reference to the tuples in a relation?

A. Index   **B.** Reference
C. Assertion   **D.** Timestamp
E. None of these

Q.22 What type of relationship exists between a Teacher table and a Class table?

A. One-to-many   **B.** Many-to-many
C. One-to-one   **D.** Two- to- two
E. All of the above

Q.23 Primitive operations common to all record management system include _________.

A. Print   **B.** Sort
C. Look up   **D.** Entity
E. None of these

Q.24 The language used in application programs to request data from the DBMS is referred to as _________.

A. DML   **B.** DDL
C. VDL   **D.** SDL
E. None of these

Q.25 Arrange the following according to the size.

A. Record, field, byte, bit
B. Bit, field, byte, record
C. Field, byte, record, bit
D. Byte, bit, record, field
E. All of the above

Q.26 Aggregate functions are functions that take a _________ as input and return a single value.

A. Collection of values   **B.** Single value
C. Aggregate value   **D.** (A) & (B) Both

E. None of these

Q.27 What field type is best to store serial numbers?

A. Number   **B.** AutoNumber
C. Text   **D.** Memo
E. None of these

Q.28 What is part of a database that holds only one type of information?

A. Report   **B.** Field
C. Record   **D.** File
E. None of these

Q.29 In DBMS, all the data is stored at a _________.

A. Central   **B.** Multiple
C. RDBMS   **D.** Both (A) and (B)
E. None of these

Q.30
Which of the following is not a component of relational database?

A. Entity   **B.** Attribute
C. Table   **D.** Hierarchy
E. All of the above

// Smart Answer Sheet //

Correct Percentage of students who answered correctly. **Skipped** Percentage of students who skipped.

Q.	Ans.	Correct / Skipped	Q.	Ans.	Correct / Skipped	Q.	Ans.	Correct / Skipped	Q.	Ans.	Correct / Skipped	Q.	Ans.	Correct / Skipped	Q.	Ans.	Correct / Skipped
1	C	80.76 % / 15.36 %	6	C	84.92 % / 14.7 %	11	A	51.8 % / 44.54 %	16	C	89.41 % / 10.42 %	21	A	60.77 % / 37.98 %	26	A	67.96 % / 31.04 %
2	B	53.24 % / 45.11 %	7	B	85.23 % / 12.58 %	12	D	62.85 % / 36.4 %	17	A	51.57 % / 46.38 %	22	B	65.6 % / 31.11 %	27	B	77.01 % / 22.21 %
3	D	51.34 % / 39.88 %	8	C	69.5 % / 30.11 %	13	B	55.62 % / 39.29 %	18	B	60.51 % / 39.15 %	23	C	58.65 % / 33.48 %	28	B	89.72 % / 10.03 %
4	C	81.33 % / 10.81 %	9	B	47.38 % / 46.64 %	14	B	44.3 % / 54.35 %	19	C	51.76 % / 47.42 %	24	A	54.39 % / 39.19 %	29	A	45.62 % / 40.97 %
5	C	84.5 % / 11.71 %	10	A	69.01 % / 30.57 %	15	C	53.53 % / 42.52 %	20	A	41.79 % / 53.07 %	25	A	79.38 % / 18.57 %	30	D	67.07 % / 32.16 %

//Hints and Solutions//

1. MS – Access is a general-purpose database management system (DBMS) is a software system designed to allow the definition, creation, querying, update, and administration of databases. Well-known DBMSs include MySQL, Microsoft SQL Server, Oracle, SAP, etc.

Hence the correct option is (C).

2. Microsoft Access is a database management system (DBMS) from the Microsoft Office package that combines the relational Microsoft Jet Database Engine with a graphical user interface and software-development tools.

Hence the correct option is (B).

3. Hardware support teams only maintain the hardware in which DBMS works. Rest all, that is ultimate users, administrators, and database designers use DBMS.

Hence the correct option is (D).

4. An RDBMS has a key that is common to many database files within an RDBMS. With the help of this common key, the RDBMS program can hop and jump from one file to another in no time and thus gather data with ease. In a DBMS, this utility is not available.

Hence the correct option is (C).

5. In DBMS, a defined field can have a fixed length defined by data type. In database systems, a field can have a fixed or a variable length. Fixed length means having a set length that never varies. A variable-length field is one whose length can be different in each record, depending on what data is stored in the field.

Hence the correct option is (C).

6. RDBMS include Oracle Database, MySQL, Microsoft SQL Server, and IBM DB2. Some of these programs support non-relational databases, but they are primarily used for relational database management.

Hence, the correct option is (C).

7. An entity set that does not possess sufficient attributes to form a primary key is called a weak entity set. One that does have a primary key is called a strong entity set.

Hence, the correct option is (B).

8. A DBMS that keeps its physical structure hidden from the user is known as a transparent DBMS. A DBMS may provide a various· levels of transparency. However, they all participate in the same overall objective: to make the use of the distributed database, equivalent to that of a centralized database.

We can identify four main types of transparency in a DBMS:

- Distribution transparency
- Transaction transparency
- Performance transparency;
- DBMS transparency.

Hence, the correct option is (C).

9. The data stored in a database must be independent of the applications that access the database. Any change in the physical structure of a database must not have any impact on how the data is being accessed by external applications. This rule is called Physical Data Independence. This is the first major rule of DBMS.

Hence, the correct option is (B).

10. The logical data in a database must be independent of its user's view (application). Any change in logical data must not affect the applications using it. This rule is called Logical Data Independence. For example, if two tables are merged or one is split into two different tables, there should be no impact or change on the user application. This is one of the most difficult rules to apply. This is the second major rule of DBMS.

Hence, the correct option is (A).

11. In Distribution Independence, the end-user must not be able to see that the data is distributed over various locations. Users should always get the impression that the data is located at one site only. This rule has been regarded as the foundation of distributed database systems. This is the third major rule of DBMS.

Hence, the correct option is (A).

12. A database must be independent of the application that uses it. All its integrity constraints can be independently modified without the need for any change in the application. This rule makes a database-independent of the front-end application and its interface.

Hence, the correct option is (D).

13. Related fields in a database are grouped to form a data record. A record is a collection of fields, possibly of different data types, typically in fixed number and sequence. In the structure of a database, the part consisting of several uniquely named components called data fields. Several data records make up a data file, and several data files make up a database.

Hence, the correct option is (B).

14. We can define a super key as a set of those keys that identify a row or a tuple uniquely. The word super denotes the superiority of a key. Thus, a super key is the superset of a key known as a Candidate key. Here the "ID" is the only attribute that can be taken as a key. Other attributes are not uniquely identified.

Hence, the correct option is (B).

15. A primary key is a special relational database table column (or combination of columns) designated to uniquely identify all table records. A primary key's main feature is that it must contain a unique value for each row of data and it cannot contain null values.

Hence, the correct option is (C).

16. Databases in MS Access are composed of four objects that is tables, queries, forms, and reports. Together, these objects allow you to enter, store, analyze, and compile your data however you want. Query in the database object in MS Access stores a question about the data in the database.

Hence, the correct option is (C).

17. When there are more than one candidate key then anomalies are generated even when the relation is in 3NF. A relation is in BCNF if, and only if, every determinant is a candidate key. Boyce-Codd's normal form is a special case of 3NF.

Hence, the correct option is (A).

18. An expression is any legal combination of symbols and characters that results a value. An expression builder is an access tool that controls an expression box for entering an expression.

Hence, the correct option is (B).

19. DML refers to the tools used to add, update and access the data within a database, including things like artists, albums, and so on in our music database example. DML is a categorization of existing SQL commands. DML commands include SELECT, INSERT, UPDATE, and DELETE.

Hence, the correct option is (C).

20. The conceptual view is where it describes what data are actually stored in the database. It contains information about the entire database in terms of small and simple structures.

Hence, the correct option is (A).

21. An index of an attribute of a relation is a data structure that allows the database management system to find those tuples in the relation that have a specified value for that attribute efficiently, without scanning through all the tuples of the relation.

Hence, the correct option is (A).

22. A many-to-many relationship occurs when multiple records in a table are associated with multiple records in another table. For example, a relationship exists between a Teacher table and a Class table.

Hence, the correct option is (B).

23. Primitive operations common to all record management systems include look up. The Database look up allows you to look up for the values in a database table. The look up values are added as new fields onto the stream.

Hence, the correct option is (C).

24. A data manipulation language (DML) is a computer programming language used for adding (inserting), deleting, and modifying (updating) data in a database. And it is the language used in application programs to request data from the DBMS. A DML is often a sub-language of a broader database language such as SQL, with the DML comprising some of the operators in the language.

Hence, the correct option is (A).

25. The descending order or correct order among the following is Record, field, byte, bit. 8 bit = 1 byte and collection of bytes made field and collection of fields made record.

Hence, the correct option is (A).

26. An aggregate function receives a set or collection of values for each argument (such as the values of a column) and returns a single-value result for the set of input values.

Hence, the correct option is (A).

27. AutoNumber field type is best to store serial numbers. AutoNumber is a type of data used in Microsoft Access tables to generate an automatically incremented numeric counter.

Hence, the correct option is (B).

28. The field is part of a database that holds only one type of information. Field (also called data member or member variable) is the data encapsulated within a class or object.

Hence, the correct option is (B).

29. A central database is a database that is located, stored, and maintained in a single location. This location is most often a central computer or database system, for example, a desktop or server CPU, or a mainframe computer.

Hence, the correct option is (A).

30. Except, hierarchy all other, are components of relational database. The traditional storage of data that is organized by customer, stored in separate folders in filing cabinets is an example of hierarchy type of 'database' system.

Hence, the correct option is (D).

Q.1 Which one is considered Indias first supercomputer?
A. Aditya
B. Vikram-100
C. Param 8000
D. Shastra T
E. None of these

Q.2 Which of the following is not an example of a Word Processor?
A. IBM Lotus Symphony
B. Microsoft Excel
C. Google Docs
D. Microsoft Word
E. Notepad

Q.3 The invention of _______ led to the third generation of computers.
A. Vacuum tubes
B. Very Large Scale Integration (VLSI)
C. Transistors
D. Integrated chips
E. None of these

Q.4 The fifth-generation computer is also known as:
A. Knowledge information processing system
B. Very large scale integration (VLSI)
C. Large scale integration (LSI)
D. Both (A) and (B)
E. None of above

Q.5 Who programmed the first computer game "Spacewar" in 1962?
A. Steve Russell
B. Konrad Zuse
C. Alan Emtage
D. Tim Berners-Lee
E. None of these

Q.6 Who is known as the father of supercomputing?
A. David J. Brown
B. Gene Amdahl
C. Adam Dunkels
D. Seymour Cray
E. None of these

Q.7 Microprocessors as switching devices are for which generation computers:
A. First Generation
B. Second Generation
C. Third Generation
D. Fourth Generation
E. Fifth Generation

Q.8 Which generation computer is IBM 1401?
A. First Generation Computer
B. Second Generation Computer
C. Third Generation Computer
D. Fourth Generation Computer
E. Fifth Generation Computer

Q.9 The computer size was very large in _________.
A. First Generation
B. Second Generation
C. Third Generation
D. Fourth Generation
E. Fifth Generation

Q.10 Second Generation computers were developed during
A. 1949 to 1955
B. 1956 to 1963
C. 1965 to 1970
D. 1970 to 1990
E. 1970 to 1996

Q.11 The chief component of the first-generation computers was-
A. Transistors
B. Vacuum Tubes and Valves
C. Integrated Circuits
D. (A) and (B) both
E. None of above

Q.12 The term 'Pentium' is related to -
A. DVD
B. Hard Disk
C. Microprocessor
D. Mouse
E. RAM

Q.13 What is the chief feature of the modern-day computer system?
A. High speed
B. All devices becoming solid state
C. High efficiency
D. Low efficiency
E. All of these

Q.14 Which one of the following is the odd man out, insofar as the Fifth Generation is concerned?
A. HDD of 1.2 GB or less
B. Core i-7 CPU
C. IPS Technology for VDU
D. Cloud computing
E. None of these

Q.15 MS-DOS is a _______ operating system.
A. User-Friendly Graphical
B. Graphical User Interface
C. Real-Time GUI
D. Command Line Interface
E. A and B both

Q.16 The abacus was believed to have been first used around 5000 B.C. in which country?
A. Japan
B. China
C. Germany
D. France
E. Iraq

Q.17 Which one of the following is not the jargon of the computers of the Fourth Generation?
A. simulation
B. Android-based hardware
C. Parallel computing

D. visualization

E. None of these

Q.18 Which one of the following is not a feature of the computers of the Third Generation?

A. The third generation was started with the invention of Integrated Circuits, known chips.

B. Small scale integrated circuits had 10 transistors per chip and medium scale integrated circuits had 100 transistors per chip.

C. These computers replaced transistors with Integrated Circuits.

D. Third-generation machines were fast and expensive.

E. None of these

Q.19 Which one of the following is not an example of the Second Generation of Computers?

A. Core i-5

B. UNIVAC 1108

C. CDC 3600

D. IBM 1401

E. Core i-3

Q.20 ENIAC stands for _________.

A. Electronic Numerical Integrator And Computer

B. Electronic Numerical Integrator And Calculator

C. Electronic Numerical Integrator Automatic Computer

D. Electronic Numerical Integrator Automatic Calculator

E. None of these

Q.21 Babbage designed the following.

A. Difference Engine : 1822 AD

B. Analytical Engine : 1833 AD

C. Pascaline : 1856 AD

D. Only (A) and (B)

E. None of the above

Q.22 In this generation Time sharing, Real-time, Networks, Distributed Operating System was used.

A. 1st   **B.** 2nd   **C.** 4th   **D.** 5th

E. 6th

Q.23 Computers of the Fifth Generation do not include the-

A. scientific calculator

B. laptab

C. ultrabook

D. (A) and (B) both

E. None of these

Q.24 The second generation of computers used-

A. transistors   **B.** vacuum tubes

C. VLSI   **D.** integrated circuit

E. None of these

Q.25 Who invented the punch card?

A. Charles Babbage

B. Semen Korsakov

C. Herman Hollerith

D. Joseph Marie Jacquard

E. None of the above

Q.26 What is Michelangelo in the world of computers?

A. A High Quality Designer Software

B. A virus

C. A type of circuit

D. A malicious

E. None of the these

Q.27 A term in computer terminology is a change in technology a computer is/was being used.

A. development   **B.** generation

C. advancement   **D.** growth

E. None of these

Q.28 Which was the first electronic digital programmable computing device?

A. Analytical Engine   **B.** Difference Engine

C. Colossus   **D.** ENIAC

E. None of these

Q.29 _________ is used as a programming language in first generation computers?

A. FORTRAN   **B.** COBOL

C. BASIC   **D.** Machine Language

E. None of these

Q.30 The main body of the computer machine is divided into two main parts?

A. CPU and Peripherals

B. External parts and internal part

C. Hardware and CPU

D. Hardware and software

E. None of these

// Smart Answer Sheet //

Correct Percentage of students who answered correctly.   **Skipped** Percentage of students who skipped.

Q.	Ans.	Correct / Skipped	Q.	Ans.	Correct / Skipped	Q.	Ans.	Correct / Skipped	Q.	Ans.	Correct / Skipped	Q.	Ans.	Correct / Skipped	Q.	Ans.	Correct / Skipped
1	C	61.93 % / 34.56 %	6	D	46.58 % / 52.96 %	11	B	62.45 % / 35.99 %	16	E	55.53 % / 35.39 %	21	D	61.41 % / 37.7 %	26	B	54.6 % / 32.97 %
2	B	55.78 % / 43.17 %	7	D	61.44 % / 30.89 %	12	C	41.06 % / 57.83 %	17	B	50.74 % / 35.13 %	22	D	60.05 % / 38.65 %	27	B	46.07 % / 42.7 %
3	D	64.81 % / 33.21 %	8	B	53.28 % / 44.77 %	13	B	51.93 % / 37.37 %	18	D	42.07 % / 37.59 %	23	A	45.1 % / 44.04 %	28	D	59.72 % / 37.88 %
4	A	68.85 % / 30.19 %	9	A	60.34 % / 35.65 %	14	A	64.85 % / 31.16 %	19	A	57.54 % / 30.59 %	24	A	46.99 % / 40.53 %	29	D	57.33 % / 32.08 %
5	A	49.57 % / 31.9 %	10	B	64.38 % / 35.39 %	15	D	65.23 % / 33.88 %	20	A	57.94 % / 37.5 %	25	C	44.19 % / 55.43 %	30	D	49.97 % / 48.11 %

//Hints and Solutions//

1. Supercomputer PARAM 8000 (made by the Centre for Development of Advanced Computing (C-DAC)) was launched on July 1, 1991 is considered India's first supercomputer. PARAM 8000, India's 1st Giga-scale supercomputer in 1990. PARAM 10000, 100 Gigaflop supercomputer in 1998.

Hence, the correct option is (C).

2. Microsoft Excel is a spreadsheet program used to store and retrieve numerical data in a grid format of columns and rows. Excel is ideal for entering, calculating and analyzing company data such as sales figures, sales taxes or commissions.

Hence, the correct option is (B).

3. The period of third generation was from 1965-1971. The computers of third generation used Integrating Circuits in place of transistors. The invention of integrated circuit brought us the third generation of computers. With this invention computers became smaller, more powerful more reliable and they are able to run many different programs at the same time.

Hence, the correct option is (D).

4. The fifth-generation computer is also known as the Knowledge information processing system. The Fifth Generation Computer Systems (FGCS) was an initiative by Japan's Ministry of International Trade and Industry (MITI), begun in 1982, to create computers using massively parallel computing and logic programming.

Hence, the correct option is (A).

5. "Spacewar" is a space combat video game developed in 1962 by Steve Russell. The game features two spaceships, "the needle" and "the wedge", engaged in a dogfight while manoeuvring in the gravity well of a star.

Hence, the correct option is (A).

6. Seymour Roger Cray was an American electrical engineer and supercomputer architect who designed a series of computers that were the fastest in the world for decades. Seymour Cray is universally known as the father of supercomputing. This article describes some of Cray's many contributions to supercomputing as he worked in five different corporate environments from 1951 until his death.

Hence, the correct option is (D).

7. Microprocessors further revolutionized the development of computers. Personal microcomputers were possible due to the microprocessors. The first microprocessor called Intel 4004 was developed by American Intel Corporation in 1971. Microprocessors are used in the computers of fourth generation computers.

Hence, the correct option is (D).

8. IBM 1401 is Second Generation Computer. The IBM 1401 is a variable word length decimal computer that was announced by IBM on October 5, 1959. 1401 was withdrawn on February 8, 1971. t was aimed at replacing unit record equipment for processing data stored on punched cards and at providing peripheral services for larger computers.

Hence, the correct option is (B).

9. The computer size was very large in First Generation, and it makes use of more than 1000s of vacuum tubes which need to be a lot of space made in the form of the gigantic size. The first computer, built-in 1946 with vacuum tubes, was called ENIAC, or Electronic Numerical Integrator and Computer.

Hence, the correct option is (A).

10. During the period from 1956 to 1963, the second generation of computers was developed. Second-generation computers emerged with the development of Transistors. The transistor was invented in 1947 by three scientists J. Bardeen, H.W. Brattain and W. Shockley.

Hence, the correct option is (B).

11. The computers of first-generation used vacuum tubes as the basic components for memory and circuitry for CPU (Central Processing Unit). First-generation computers used vacuum tubes and valves as their main electronic component. Vacuum Tubes were invented by Lee De Forest in 1908.

Hence, the correct option is (B).

12. Pentium is a brand used for a series of x86 architecture-compatible microprocessors produced by Intel since 1993. The term 'Pentium' is related to Microprocessor. The Pentium is a widely-used personal computer microprocessor from the Intel Corporation.

Hence, the correct option is (C).

13. The striking feature of modern computer systems is that the dependence on rotating devices is becoming less by the day. The traditional HDD is being replaced by a solid-state drive which can store data up to a few terabytes. This is a major development in the field of computer-oriented technology. The machines of the previous generation were also fast. True, the speed of modern machines has increased but the major breakthrough areas are high definition display, cloud computing, Artificial Intelligence and solid-state devices inside the computer CPU.

Hence, the correct option is (B).

14. A hard disk drive (HDD), hard disk, hard drive, or fixed disk is an electromechanical data storage device that stores and retrieves digital data using magnetic storage and one or more rigid rapidly rotating platters coated with magnetic material.

Hence, the correct option is (A).

15. The short form for Microsoft Disk Operating System, MS-DOS is a non-graphical command line operating system derived from 86-DOS that was created for IBM compatible computers. It is a command-line-based system, where all commands are entered in text form and there is no graphical user interface.

Hence, the correct option is (D).

16. The earliest recorded calculating device is the abacus. Used as a simple computing device for performing arithmetic, the abacus

most likely appeared first in Babylonia (now Iraq) over 5000 years ago.

Hence, the correct option is (E).

17. Android-based hardware was developed in the Fifth Generation. Multimedia, visualization, parallel computing were developed in the Fourth generation but advanced multimedia files were developed in the Fifth Generation.

Hence, the correct option is (B).

18. Third generation machines were faster and expensive. The main features of the third-generation computers were that they; used Integrated Circuits, reliable in comparison to the previous two generations, smaller in size, generated less heat, faster in terms of speed, lesser maintenance, still costly, A.C needed, and consumed lesser electricity.

Hence, the correct option is (D).

19. The machines based on Core i-5 CPU belong to the Fifth Generation. A transistor computer, now often called a second-generation computer, is a computer that uses discrete transistors instead of vacuum tubes. The first generation of electronic computers used vacuum tubes, which generated large amounts of heat, was bulky and unreliable.

Hence, the correct option is (A).

20. ENIAC (Electronic Numerical Integrator And Computer) was the world's first general-purpose computer. ENIAC was designed and built for the United States Army to calculate artillery firing tables. John Mauchly and J. Presper Eckert built the machine at the University of Pennsylvania at the behest of the U.S. military.

Hence, the correct option is (A).

21. Babbage designed Difference Engine in 1822. He built it to calculate mathematical tables. Babbage also designed Analytical Engine in 1833. The Analytical Engine had almost all the parts that a modern computer has. Its design was very much similar to that of the modern computer.

Hence, the correct option is (D).

22. The fourth generation of computers is marked by the use of Very Large Scale Integrated (VLSI) circuits. In this generation Time sharing, Real-time, Networks, Distributed Operating System was used.

Hence, the correct option is (D).

23. The first scientific calculator that included all of the basic ideas above was the programmable Hewlett-Packard HP-9100A, released in 1968 and this is the time of third-generation computers.

Hence, the correct option is (A).

24. A transistor computer, now often called a second-generation computer, is a computer that uses discrete transistors instead of vacuum tubes. The second generation of computers of the 1950s and 1960s had circuit boards filled with individual transistors and magnetic core memory.

Hence, the correct option is (A).

25. Herman Hollerith was an American inventor who developed an electromechanical punched card tabulator to assist in summarizing information and, later, accounting.

Hence, the correct option is (C).

26. The Michelangelo virus is a computer virus first discovered on 4 February 1991 in Australia. The virus was designed to infect DOS systems but did not engage the operating system or make any OS calls.

Hence, the correct option is (B).

27. Generation in computer terminology is a change in technology a computer was being used. The term is used to distinguish between various hardware technologies.

Hence, the correct option is (B).

28. The US-built ENIAC (Electronic Numerical Integrator and Computer) was the first electronic programmable computer built in the US. On February 15, 1946, the Army revealed the existence of ENIAC to the public. In a special ceremony, the Army introduced ENIAC and its hardware inventors Dr. John Mauchly and J. Presper Eckert.

Hence, the correct option is (D).

29. A first-generation (programming) language (1GL) is a grouping of programming languages that are machine level languages used to program first-generation computers.

Hence, the correct option is (D).

30. Hardware includes the physical features, which are every part that you can either see or touch, for example, monitor, case, keyboard, mouse, and printer. The part which activates the physical components is called software. It includes the features that responsible for directing the work to the hardware. The software can be divided into other programs and data.

Hence, the correct option is (D).

Q.1 What type of commands are required to perform various tasks in DOS?

A. Internal commands   **B.** External commands

C. Valuable commands   **D.** Primary commands

E. None of the above

Q.2 If you want to execute more than one program at a time, the systems software you are using must be capable of:

A. word processing   **B.** virtual memory

C. compiling   **D.** multitasking

E. None of the above

Q.3 What type of scheduling is round-robin scheduling?

A. Linear data scheduling

B. Non-linear data scheduling

C. Preemptive scheduling

D. Non-preemptive scheduling

E. None of the above

Q.4 What is the work of Round-robin scheduling?

A. It allows interactive tasks quicker access to the processor.

B. It is quite complex to implement.

C. It gives each task the same chance at the processor.

D. It allows processor-bound tasks more time in the processor.

E. None of the above

Q.5 What is the name of the system which deals with the running of the actual computer and not with the programming problems?

A. Operating system   **B.** Systems program

C. Object program   **D.** Source program

E. None of the above

Q.6 What is the initial value of the semaphore to allow only one of the many processes to enter their critical section?

A. 8   **B.** 1

C. 16   **D.** 0

E. None of the above

Q.7 Four necessary conditions for deadlock to exist are: mutual exclusion, no-preemption, circular wait and-

A. hold and wait

B. deadlock avoidance

C. race around condition

D. buffer overflow

E. None of the above

Q.8 If you do not know which version of MS-DOS you are working with, which command will you use after having booted your operating system?

A. FORMAT command

B. DIR command

C. VER command

D. DISK command

E. None of the above

Q.9 A partitioned data set is most used for-

A. a program or source library

B. storing program data

C. storing backup information

D. storing ISAM files

E. None of the above

Q.10 What is Page-map table?

A. It is a data file.

B. It is a directory.

C. It is used for address translation.

D. (A) and (B) both

E. None of the above

Q.11 The main function of the dispatcher (the portion of the process scheduler) is ________.

A. swapping a process to the disk

B. assigning ready process to the CPU

C. suspending some of the processes when the CPU load is high

D. bring processes from the disk to the main memory

E. None of the above

Q.12 Which of the following commands creates an emergency repair disk for Windows NT 4.0?

A. BAT

B. EXE

C. EXE/S

D. ADD/REMOVE program

E. None of the above

Q.13 When a computer is first turned on or restarted, a special type of absolute loader is executed, called a-

A. Compile and Go loader

B. Boot loader

C. Bootstrap loader

D. Relating loader

E. None of the above

Q.14 Which of the following scheduling algorithms is preemptive scheduling?

A. FCFS Scheduling

B. SJF Scheduling

C. Network Scheduling

D. SRTF Scheduling

E. Priority Based Scheduling

Q.15 Which program runs first after booting the computer and loading the GUI?

A. Desktop Manager   **B.** File Manager

C. Windows Explorer   **D.** Authentication

E. None of these

Q.16 Which of the following is an example of a Real Time Operating System?

A. MAC
B. MS-DOS
C. Windows 10
D. Process Control
E. None of the above

Q.17 In MS-DOS, relocatable object files and load modules have extensions:

A. .OBJ and .COM or .EXE, respectively
B. .COM and .OBJ, respectively
C. .EXE and .OBJ, respectively
D. .DAS and .EXE, respectively
E. None of the above

Q.18 The state transition initiated by the user process itself in an operating system is:

A. Bock
B. Dispatch
C. Wake up
D. Timer run out
E. None of the above

Q.19 Which of the following operating system runs on the server?

A. Batch OS
B. Distributed OS
C. Real-time OS
D. Network OS
E. None of the above

Q.20 SSTF stands for _______.

A. Shortest Signal Time First
B. Shortest Seek Time First
C. System Seek Time First
D. System Shortest Time First
E. None of the above

Q.21 What type of memory stores data in a swap file on a hard drive?

A. Secondary memory
B. Virtual memory
C. Low memory
D. RAM
E. None of the above

Q.22 The characteristic of Feed back queue is-

A. Are very easy to implement
B. Dispatch tasks according to execution characteristics
C. Are used to favor real-time tasks
D. Require manual intervention to implement properly
E. None of the above

Q.23 In which addressing mode the operand is given explicitly in the instruction?

A. Absolute mode
B. Immediate mode
C. Indirect mode
D. Index mode
E. None of the above

Q.24 The technique, for sharing the time of a computer among several jobs. Which switches jobs so rapidly such that each job appears to have the computer to itself:

A. Time-sharing
B. Time out
C. Time domain
D. FIFO
E. None of the above

Q.25 What is Microsoft window?

A. Operating system
B. Graphics program
C. Word Processing
D. Database program
E. All of the above

Q.26 Poor response times are caused by-

A. Processor busy
B. High I/O rate
C. High paging rates
D. (A), (B) and (C)
E. None of the above

Q.27 How many types of buffer overflow in the operating system?

A. Two
B. Three
C. Six
D. Seven
E. Five

Q.28 A form of code that uses more than one process and processor, possibly of different type, and that may on occasions have more than one process or processor active at the same time, is known as?

A. multiprogramming
B. multithreading
C. broadcasting
D. time sharing
E. None of the above

Q.29 Which of the following algorithms is used to avoid deadlock?

A. Dynamic Programming algorithm
B. Primality algorithms
C. Banker's algorithm
D. Deadlock algorithm
E. None of the above

Q.30 Which of the following method is used to prevent threads or processes from accessing a single resource?

A. PCB
B. Semaphore
C. Job Scheduler
D. Non-Contiguous Memory Allocation
E. None of the above

// Smart Answer Sheet //

Correct — Percentage of students who answered correctly. **Skipped** — Percentage of students who skipped.

Q.	Ans.	Correct / Skipped	Q.	Ans.	Correct / Skipped	Q.	Ans.	Correct / Skipped	Q.	Ans.	Correct / Skipped	Q.	Ans.	Correct / Skipped	Q.	Ans.	Correct / Skipped
1	B	59.93 % / 32.9 %	6	B	44.3 % / 48.48 %	11	B	48.49 % / 47.56 %	16	D	58.34 % / 40.48 %	21	B	57.89 % / 37.53 %	26	D	83.61 % / 10.85 %
2	D	59.13 % / 33.53 %	7	A	52.42 % / 42.22 %	12	B	47.95 % / 42.27 %	17	A	51.34 % / 44.18 %	22	B	68.77 % / 30.71 %	27	A	61.23 % / 37.43 %
3	C	62.36 % / 36.71 %	8	C	61.96 % / 36.58 %	13	C	66.71 % / 30.58 %	18	A	63.83 % / 35.31 %	23	B	43.4 % / 37.86 %	28	B	62.99 % / 34.37 %
4	C	50.34 % / 40.73 %	9	A	58.92 % / 39.35 %	14	D	56.98 % / 30.4 %	19	D	66.84 % / 31.89 %	24	A	31.4 % / 67.65 %	29	C	45.11 % / 49.94 %
5	B	55.32 % / 39.51 %	10	C	53.7 % / 39.68 %	15	D	64.09 % / 33.55 %	20	B	68.31 % / 30.73 %	25	A	88.85 % / 10.95 %	30	B	56.46 % / 35.32 %

//Hints and Solutions//

1. External commands are required to perform various tasks in DOS. External commands are powerful. They help fix problems, improve performance, and perform other actions as well. External commands usually have higher resource requirements than internal commands. Keeping them in separate files, separated from internal commands, helps to reduce the load on Windows. They can also be added to Windows whenever needed by copying the external command's file to the computer.

Hence, the correct option is (B).

2. If you want to execute more than one program at a time, the systems software you are using must be capable of multitasking. Multitasking, in an operating system, is allowing a user to perform more than one computer task (such as the operation of an application program) at a time.

Hence, the correct option is (D).

3. Round-robin scheduling is a preemptive scheduling algorithm in which a specific time is provided to execute each process. This specific time is called time-slice. Round-robin is one of the algorithms employed by process and network schedulers in computing. As the term is generally used, time slices are assigned to each process in equal portions and in circular order, handling all processes without priority.

Hence, the correct option is (C).

4. Round-robin scheduling gives each task the same chance at the processor. Round Robin is a CPU scheduling algorithm where each process is assigned a fixed time slot in a cyclic way. It is simple, easy to implement, and starvation-free as all processes get a fair share of CPU. One of the most commonly used techniques in CPU scheduling is a core.

Hence, the correct option is (C).

5. Systems program deals with the running of the actual computer and not with the programming problems. A computer program is a collection of instructions that performs a specific task when executed by a computer.

Hence, the correct option is (B).

6. The initial value of the semaphore that allows only one of the many processes to enter their critical sections, is 1. For signaling, the semaphore is initialized to 0; for mutual exclusion, the initial value is 1; for multiplexing, the initial value is a positive number greater than 1.

Hence, the correct option is (B).

7. A deadlock in OS is a situation where two or more processes are blocked. Conditions for Deadlock- Mutual Exclusion, Hold and Wait, No preemption, Circular wait. These 4 conditions must hold simultaneously for the occurrence of deadlock.

Hence, the correct option is (A).

8. VER command is used after booting the operating system when the version of MS-DOS being worked upon is not known.

In computing, ver is a command in various DOS, FlexOS, OS/2, and Microsoft Windows command-line interpreters such as COMMAND.COM, cmd.exe, and 4DOS/4NT. It prints the name and version of the operating system or the command shell.

Hence, the correct option is (C).

9. A partitioned data set is most used for a program or source library. A partitioned data set (PDS) is a data set containing multiple members, each of which holds a separate sub-data set, similar to a directory in other types of file systems.

Hence, the correct option is (A).

10. Page-map table is used for address translation. A page table is the data structure used by a virtual memory system in a computer operating system to store the mapping between virtual addresses and physical addresses. Virtual addresses are used by the program executed by the accessing process, while physical addresses are used by the hardware, or more specifically, by the RAM subsystem. The page table is a key component of virtual address translation which is necessary to access data in memory.

Hence, the correct option is (C).

11. The main function of the dispatcher is assigning the ready processes to the CPU. CPU scheduler selects a process among the processes that are ready to execute and allocates CPU to one of them. Short-term schedulers, also known as dispatchers, make the decision of which process to execute next.

Hence, the correct option is (B).

12. There are the following steps to repair disk in windows NT 4.0:

Step 1: Go to the search button in windows NT 4.0, then type Command Prompt.

Step 2: Then type "RDISK.EXE" and press enter.

Step 3: Then open a pop-up window. This pop-up window will update the emergency repair disk.

Hence, the correct option is (B).

13. A bootstrap loader is a program that resides in the computer's EPROM, ROM, or other non-volatile memory. It is automatically executed by the processor when turning on the computer. A bootloader, also known as a boot program or bootstrap loader, is special operating system software that loads into the working memory of a computer after start-up.

Hence, the correct option is (C).

14. Shortest Remaining Time First (SRTF) scheduling is preemptive scheduling. In this scheduling, the process that has the shortest processing time left is executed first. Since the currently executing process is the one with the shortest amount of time remaining by definition, and since that time should only reduce as execution progresses, the process will either run until it completes or get preempted if a new process is added that requires a smaller amount of time.

Hence, the correct option is (D).

15. The authentication program is run first after booting the computer and loading the GUI. Authentication is a process of verifying the person or device. For example, when you log in to Facebook, you enter a username and password.

Hence, the correct option is (D).

16. Process control is a best example of a Real time operating system. The function of the realtime operation system is to control resources in the system shared by application tasks including input/output devices, computer memory, and the CPU itself.

Hence, the correct option is (D).

17. In MS-DOS, relocatable object files and load modules have extensions is .OBJ and .COM or .EXE, respectively.

.OBJ: OBJ is a geometry definition file format first developed by Wavefront Technologies for its Advanced Visualizer animation package.

.COM: The domain name com is a top-level domain in the Domain Name System of the Internet. Its name is derived from the word commercial, indicating its original intended purpose for domains registered by commercial organizations.

.EXE: EXE is a file extension for an executable file format. An executable is a file that contains a program - that is, a particular kind of file that is capable of being executed or run as a program in the computer. An executable file can be run by a program in Microsoft DOS or Windows through a command or a double click.

Hence, the correct option is (A).

18. The state transition initiated by the user process itself in an operating system is block. A block is a contiguous set of bits or bytes that forms an identifiable unit of data. The term is used in database management, word processing, and network communication. It is a multiple of an operating system block, which is the smallest amount of data that can be retrieved from storage or memory.

Hence, the correct option is (A).

19. The network operating system runs on a server. This operating system has some functions that work to connect local area networks and computers. A network operating system (NOS) is an operating system that manages network resources: essentially, an operating system that includes special functions for connecting computers and devices into a local area network (LAN). The NOS manages multiple requests (inputs) concurrently and provides the security necessary in a multiuser environment.

Hence, the correct option is (D).

20. SSTF stands for Shortest Seek Time First. In the SSTF algorithm, that request is executed first, whose seek time is the shortest. Shortest seek time first is a secondary storage scheduling algorithm to determine the motion of the disk's arm and head in servicing read and write requests.

Hence, the correct option is (B).

21. A swap file is a space on a hard disk used as the virtual memory extension of a computer's real memory (RAM). Having a swap file allows your computer's operating system to pretend that you have more RAM than you actually do. The least recently used files in RAM can be "swapped out" to your hard disk until they are needed later so that new files can be "swapped in" to RAM.

Hence, the correct option is (B).

22. Feed back queue dispatch tasks according to execution characteristics. Multilevel Feedback Queue Scheduling (MLFQ) keep analyzing the behaviour (time of execution) of processes and according to which it changes its priority. In the last queue, processes are scheduled in FCFS manner. A process in a lower priority queue can only execute only when higher priority queues are empty.

Hence, the correct option is (B).

23. In immediate addressing mode, the operand is a part of the instruction. There is no address field as the operand is a part of the instruction. In direct address mode, the effective address of the operand is equal to the address part of the instruction, that is, the address part of the instruction points to the memory location containing the operand.

Hence, the correct option is (B).

24. The technique of sharing computer time between multiple jobs, which switches jobs so rapidly that each job appears to have its own computer, called time sharing. Time sharing refers to the allocation of computer resources in time slots to several programs simultaneously. For example a mainframe computer that has many users logged on to it. Each user uses the resources of the mainframe -i.e. memory, CPU etc.

Hence, the correct option is (A).

25. Microsoft Windows, also called Windows and Windows OS, computer operating system (OS) developed by Microsoft Corporation to run personal computers (PCs).

The first version of Windows, released in 1985, was simply a GUI offered as an extension of Microsoft's existing disk operating system, or MS-DOS. Based in part on licensed concepts that Apple Inc. had used for its Macintosh System Software, Windows for the first time allowed DOS users to visually navigate a virtual desktop opening graphical displaying the contents of electronic folders and files with the click of a mouse button rather than typing commands and directory paths at a text prompt. Microsoft Windows is available in the market in 32-bits and 64-bits

Hence, the correct option is (A).

26. Poor response times are usually caused by Process busy,High I/O rates and High paging rates. Poor response times. We are having intermittent performance issues with our new API where the response time can be from 300 ms up to 20 seconds.

Hence, the correct option is (D).

27. There are two types of buffer-overflows: heap-based and stack-based. A heap overflow condition is a buffer overflow, where the buffer that can be overwritten is allocated in the heap portion of memory, generally meaning that the buffer was allocated using a routine such as malloc(). A stack-based overflow is one in which a stack, implicitly accessed by most operations, is a fundamental part of the programming model.

Hence, the correct option is (A).

28. A form of code that uses more than one process and processor, possibly of a different type, and that may on occasions have more than one process or processor active at the same time, is known as multithreading. Multithreading is the ability of a program or an operating system process to manage its use by more than one user at a time and to even manage multiple requests by the same user without having to have multiple copies of the programming running in the computer.

Hence, the correct option is (B).

29. The Banker algorithm, sometimes referred to as the detection algorithm, is a resource allocation and deadlock avoidance algorithm developed by Edsger Dijkstra that tests for safety by simulating the allocation of predetermined maximum possible amounts of all resources, and then makes an "s-state" check to test for possible deadlock conditions for all other pending activities, before deciding whether allocation should be allowed to continue.

Hence, the correct option is (C).

30. Semaphore is an integer variable that is used to prevent threads or processes from accessing a single resource. Semaphore is simply a variable that is non-negative and shared between threads. A semaphore is a signaling mechanism, and a thread that is waiting on a semaphore can be signaled by another thread. It uses two atomic operations, wait, and signal for the process synchronization.

Hence, the correct option is (B).

Q.1 Switch to the next window from the current window _____ is used.

A. Ctrl + Tab
B. Alt + Tab
C. Alt + Right arrow
D. End Key
E. None of these

Q.2 Switch to the previous window from the current window _____ is used.

A. Alt+Shift+Tab
B. Home Key
C. Alt+Left arrow
D. Ctrl+Shift+Tab
E. Ctrl+F4

Q.3 Close the active window _____ shortcut is used.

A. Ctrl+X
B. Ctrl+W
C. Ctrl+F4
D. (B) and (C) both
E. None of these

Q.4 Restore down the size of the maximized window _____ is used.

A. Alt+F5
B. Ctrl+F5
C. Shift+F5
D. Alt+Ctrl+F5
E. Ctrl+X

Q.5 Move to a task pane from another pane in the program window clockwise direction shortcut _____ is used.

A. F3
B. F5
C. F4
D. F6
E. F8

Q.6 Move to a task pane from another pane in the program window counterclockwise direction _____ is used.

A. Alt+F6
B. Shift+F6
C. Ctrl+F6
D. Alt+Left arrow
E. None of these

Q.7 When more than one window is open, then switch to the next window from current window _____ is used.

A. Alt+Right arrow
B. Shift+F6
C. Ctrl+F6
D. Alt+F6
E. None of these

Q.8 Which of the following shortcut key is used to check spelling?

A. F3
B. F10
C. F5
D. F7
E. F11

Q.9 Capture and copy a picture of the screen to the Clipboard _____ is used.

A. PrtSc
B. Ctrl+P
C. Ctrl+F9
D. Print Window
E. Ctrl+F7

Q.10 To move from an open dialog box back to the document, for dialog boxes that support this behavior such as Find and Replace _____ is used.

A. Ctrl+F7
B. Alt+Shift+F6

C. Alt+Left arrow
D. Alt+F6
E. None of these

Q.11 The keystrokes Ctrl + I is used to:

A. Increase font size
B. Inserts a line break
C. Applies italic format to selected text
D. Indicate the text should be bold
E. None of these

Q.12 Which of the following function key activates the speller?

A. F3
B. F6
C. F7
D. F11
E. F9

Q.13 Shortcut to create new document is _____ .

A. Ctrl + F
B. Ctrl + N
C. Ctrl + O
D. Ctrl + S
E. None of these

Q.14 Shortcut to quit Microsoft Word, Powerpoint, Access, Excel etc is _____.

A. Ctrl + W
B. Ctrl + Q
C. Alt + F4
D. Alt + Q
E. None of these

Q.15 What is the correct combination of keys to find text on a document?

A. Alt + F
B. Ctrl + T
C. Ctrl + F
D. Ctrl + H
E. None of these

Q.16 Move to the next option or option group use _____.

A. Alt+tab
B. Ctrl+tab
C. Tab
D. Ctrl+right arrow
E. None of these

Q.17 To move between options in an open drop-down list, or between options in a group of options _____ is used.

A. Up and Down arrow
B. Left arrow
C. Right arrow
D. (A),(B) and (C)
E. None of these

Q.18 To select an option from the menu bar _____ is used.

A. Shift+ the letter highlighted in an option
B. Alt+ the letter highlighted in an option
C. Ctrl+ the letter highlighted in an option
D. Tab+ the letter highlighted in an option
E. None of these

Q.19 To open a selected drop-down list _____ is used.

A. Shift+Down arrow
B. Alt+Right arrow
C. Ctrl+Down arrow
D. Alt+Down arrow
E. None of these

Q.20 To close a selected drop-down list; cancel a command and close a dialog box _____ is used.
A. Esc key
B. Enter key
C. Alt key
D. Tab key
E. None of these

Q.21 What is the shortcut key to open the History box?
A. Shift+H
B. Ctrl+H
C. Alt+H
D. F3
E. None of these

Q.22 What is the shortcut key to refresh the current webpage with cache override?
A. Alt+F5
B. Ctrl+F5
C. Shift+F5
D. F5
E. None of these

Q.23 What is the shortcut key to restoring the closed tab?
A. Ctrl+Alt+T
B. Window+T
C. Ctrl+Shift+Z
D. Ctrl+Shift+T
E. None of these

Q.24 What is the shortcut key to jump to the Instant Search box?
A. Alt+S
B. Alt+Shift+S
C. Shift+E
D. Ctrl+E
E. None of these

Q.25 Which short keys is used to "Switch to parent folder" ?
A. Space
B. Backspace
C. Enter
D. Alt
E. Delete

Q.26 What is the shortcut key to open a private browsing window?
A. Alt+Shift+P
B. Ctrl+Alt+P
C. Ctrl+Shift+F
D. Ctrl+Shift+P
E. None of these

Q.27 To turn tracking changes on or off ________ is used.
A. Alt+T
B. Ctrl+Shift+T
C. Ctrl+Shift+E
D. Shift+Alt+T
E. None of these

Q.28 Mark a table of contents entry in the document _______ is used.
A. Alt+Shift+O
B. Ctrl+Shift+O
C. Ctrl+Shift+T
D. Alt+T
E. None of these

Q.29 To Insert an internal/external hyperlink in the document _______ is used.
A. Alt+K
B. Ctrl+H
C. Ctrl+K
D. Ctrl+L
E. None of these

Q.30 To move the selected text or graphics once use _______.
A. Press Ctrl+M then move the cursor press Enter
B. Press F2 then move the cursor press Enter
C. Press F6 then move the cursor press Enter

D. Ctrl+H > O, C
E. None of the above

// Smart Answer Sheet //

Correct — Percentage of students who answered correctly. **Skipped** — Percentage of students who skipped.

Q.	Ans.	Correct / Skipped	Q.	Ans.	Correct / Skipped	Q.	Ans.	Correct / Skipped	Q.	Ans.	Correct / Skipped	Q.	Ans.	Correct / Skipped	Q.	Ans.	Correct / Skipped
1	B	66.57 % / 32.92 %	6	B	49.87 % / 30.56 %	11	C	76.23 % / 13.71 %	16	C	64.33 % / 30.31 %	21	B	85.63 % / 13.16 %	26	D	77.9 % / 20.42 %
2	A	51.83 % / 33.98 %	7	C	60.44 % / 30.71 %	12	C	79.27 % / 14.14 %	17	D	86.5 % / 12.74 %	22	B	83.44 % / 12.17 %	27	C	78.4 % / 19.6 %
3	D	40.75 % / 57.54 %	8	D	82.26 % / 15.54 %	13	B	83.12 % / 13.38 %	18	B	49.32 % / 39.45 %	23	D	78.38 % / 11.99 %	28	A	53.96 % / 31.4 %
4	A	50.26 % / 39.25 %	9	A	79.88 % / 13.56 %	14	C	78.27 % / 18.68 %	19	D	88.12 % / 10.46 %	24	D	89.33 % / 10.1 %	29	C	48.58 % / 44.63 %
5	D	42.07 % / 41.71 %	10	D	53.65 % / 44.89 %	15	C	88.12 % / 11.59 %	20	A	54.56 % / 35.15 %	25	B	64.91 % / 31.53 %	30	B	40.84 % / 39.59 %

//Hints and Solutions//

1. Pressing Alt + Tab lets you switch between your open Windows. With the Alt key still pressed, tap Tab again to flip between windows, and then release the Alt key to select the current window.

Switch to the next window from the current window Alt + Tab used.

Hence, the correct option is (B).

2. Switch to the previous window from the current window Alt+Shift+Tab is used. To go past the window you want, press and hold the Alt+Shift key and tap Tab once to go back to the left.

Hence, the correct option is (A).

3. For closing the active window Ctrl+W & Ctrl+F4 both shortcuts can be used. In Microsoft Word and other word processor programs, pressing Ctrl+X cuts any text, picture, or other object that is selected.

Hence, the correct option is (D).

4. To restore a window to its unmaximized size, drag it away from the edges of the screen. If the window is fully maximized, you can double-click the title bar to restore it. You can also use the same keyboard shortcuts you used to maximize the window.

Restore down the size of the maximized window Alt+F5 is used.

Hence, the correct option is (A).

5. Move to a task pane from another pane in the program window (clockwise direction). You may need to press F6 more than once. Move to a task pane from another pane in the program window (counterclockwise direction). When more than one window is open, switch to the next window.

Move to a task pane from another pane in the program window clockwise direction F6 is used.

Hence, the correct option is (D).

6. Move to a task pane from another pane in the program window (clockwise direction). You may need to press F6 more than once. Move to a task pane from another pane in the program window (counterclockwise direction). When more than one window is open, switch to the next window.

Move to a task pane from another pane in the program window counterclockwise direction Shift+F6 is used.

Hence, the correct option is (B).

7. Reverse the direction by pressing Alt+Shift+Tab at the same time. Switches between program groups, tabs, or document windows in applications that support this feature. Reverse the direction by pressing Ctrl+Shift+Tab at the same time.

When more than one window is open, then switch to the next window from the current window Ctrl+F6 is used.

Hence, the correct option is (C).

8. Function key F7 is commonly used to spell check and grammar check a document in Microsoft programs such as Microsoft Excel, Microsoft Word, Microsoft Outlook, and other Office products.

Hence, the correct option is (D).

9. Pressing Print screen captures an image of your entire screen and copies it to the Clipboard in your computer's memory. You can then paste (Ctrl+V) the image into a document, email message, or other files.

PrtSc is used to Capture and copy a picture of the screen to the Clipboard.

Hence, the correct option is (A).

10. To move from an open dialog box back to the document, for dialog boxes that support this behavior such as Find and Replace Alt+F6 shortcut is used.

Hence, the correct option is (D).

11. Alternatively referred to as Control+I and C-i, Ctrl+I is a keyboard shortcut most often used to italicize and un-italicize text.

Hence, the correct option is (C).

12. F7 function key is used to activate the speller.

A function key is a key on a computer or terminal keyboard which can be programmed so as to cause an operating system command interpreter or application.

Hence, the correct option is (C).

13. Alternatively referred to as Control+N and C-n, Ctrl+N is a keyboard shortcut most often used to create a new document, window, workbook, or other type of file.

Shortcut to create new document is Ctrl + N.

Hence, the correct option is (B).

14. The Alt+F4 keyboard shortcut closes the current active window. However, if this is used to close application windows, depending on the application.

Shortcut to quit Microsoft Word, Powerpoint, Access, Excel etc is Alt + F4.

Hence, the correct option is (C).

15. The correct combination of keys to find text on a document Ctrl + F.

Alternatively known as Ctrl+F and C-f, Control+F is a keyboard shortcut most often used to open a find box to locate a specific character, word, or phrase in a document or web page.

Hence, the correct option is (C).

16. Move to the next option or option group use Tab.

The tab key Tab (abbreviation of tabulator key or tabular key) on a keyboard is used to advance the cursor to the next tab stop.

Hence, the correct option is (C).

17. To move between options in an open drop-down list, or between options in a group of options Up and Down arrow, Left arrow and Right arrow is used.

Hence, the correct option is (D).

18. The Alt key on a computer keyboard is used to change (alternate) the function of other pressed keys. Thus, the Alt key is a modifier key, used in a similar fashion to the Shift key.

To select an option from the menu bar Alt+ the letter highlighted in an option shortcut key is used.

Hence, the correct option is (B).

19. A drop-down list is a graphical control element, similar to a list box, that allows the user to choose one value from a list. When a drop-down list is inactive, it displays a single value. When activated, it displays (drops down) a list of values, from which the user may select one.

To open a selected drop-down list Alt+Down arrow shortcut key is used.

Hence, the correct option is (D).

20. The Esc key can often be used to get you out of dialogs or dropdown lists - it generally represents the pressing of the cancel button in these cases.

To close a selected drop-down list;

cancel a command and close a dialog box Esc key shortcut key is used.

Hence, the correct option is (A).

21. Ctrl+H is the shortcut key to open the History box.

Alternatively referred to as Control+H and C-H, Ctrl+H is a shortcut key that varies depending on the program being used. For example, in most text programs, Ctrl+H is used to find and replace text in a file. In an Internet browser, Ctrl+H may open the history.

Hence, the correct option is (B).

22. Ctrl+F5 is the shortcut key to refresh the current webpage with cache override.

The difference is that generally, F5 may use the browser cache, while Ctrl+F5 invalidates the cache and forces the browser to fetch the web page from the server.

Hence, the correct option is (B).

23. Right-click a blank space on the tab bar at the top of the window and choose "Reopen closed tab." You can also use a keyboard shortcut to accomplish this: Ctrl+Shift+T on a PC.

Ctrl+Shift+T is the shortcut key to restoring the closed tab.

Hence, the correct option is (D).

24. Ctrl+E is the shortcut key to jump to the Instant Search box. In Chrome, Edge, Firefox, Opera, and Internet Explorer, Ctrl + E focuses on the address bar, search bar, or omnibox. Using this shortcut can be helpful when you're done browsing the current page and want to type in a new address or search for something else without using the mouse.

Hence, the correct option is (D).

25. Backspace is the shortcut key for "switch to parent folder". When you enter a folder and then want to go back, you use backspace key, which can be its parent folder.

Hence, the correct option is (B).

26. Ctrl+Shift+P is the shortcut key to open a private browsing window.

From the keyboard, a private browsing session can be called up using the combination Ctrl-Shift-P (Windows) or Command-Shift-P (macOS). Alternately, a private window will open from the menu at the upper right of Firefox — three short horizontal lines — after selecting New Private Window.

Hence, the correct option is (D).

27. To turn tracking changes on or off we can use Ctrl+Shift+E.

You can turn this feature off using either a direct keyboard shortcut or the ribbon. To turn off Track Changes, on the keyboard, press Ctrl+Shift+E.

Hence, the correct option is (C).

28. Mark a table of contents entry in the document Alt+Shift+O can be used as shortcut key. Ctrl + Shift + O is use for open the Bookmarks Manager in google chrome. Ctrl-Shift-T is use for open the recently closed tab in google chrome. Alt+T is a keyboard shortcut most often used to open the Tools in the file menu.

Hence, the correct option is (A).

29. To Insert an internal/external hyperlink in the document we can use Ctrl+K as a shortcut key.

Alternatively referred to as Control+K and C-K, Ctrl+K is a keyboard shortcut that varies depending on the program used. For example, in certain programs, Ctrl+K is used to insert a hyperlink, and in some browsers, Ctrl+K focuses on the search bar.

Hence, the correct option is (C).

30. To move the selected text or graphics once press F2 then move the cursor then press Enter.

Hence, the correct option is (B).

Q.1 What is the full form of CPU?

A. Centre of Processing Unit
B. Central Processing Unit
C. Central Publication Unit
D. Central Programming Unit
E. None of these

Q.2 What does USB stand for?

A. Unique Signal Bus
B. Universal Serial Bus
C. Universal Secondary Base
D. United System Base
E. None of these

Q.3 What does EEPROM stand for?

A. Electrically Erasable Programmable Read Only Memory
B. Electronic Erasable Programmable Read Only Memory
C. Electronically Enabled Programmable Read Only Memory
D. Easily Erasable Programmable Read Only Memory
E. None of these

Q.4 UNIVAC was the first generation computer. What is its full form?

A. Universal Automatic Computer
B. Universal Array Computer
C. Unique Automatic Computer
D. Unvalued Automatic Computer
E. None of these

Q.5 What does DNS stand for?

A. Domain Name Source
B. Domain Name System
C. Description Name System
D. All of the above
E. None of these

Q.6 What does WAN stand for?

A. Wap Area Network
B. Wide Area Network
C. Wide Array Net
D. Wireless Area Network
E. None of these

Q.7 VIRUS stands for __________.

A. Vital Information Recourse Under System
B. Vital Information Resource Under Seige
C. Vital Information Resource Under Secure
D. Very Information Recourse Under System
E. None of these

Q.8 What does RAM stand for?

A. Random Access Memory
B. Read Access Memory
C. Random Attribute Memory
D. Random Applicable Memory
E. None of these

Q.9 What is the full form of MIPS?

A. Million Instructions Per Second
B. Many Instructions Per Second
C. Monthly Instructions Per Second
D. Million Inputs Per Second
E. None of these

Q.10 What does CD-ROM stand for?

A. Compactable Read Only Memory
B. Compact Data Read Only Memory
C. Compactable Delete Read Only Memory
D. Compact Disk Read-Only Memory
E. None of these

Q.11 What does DIP stand for?

A. Domain Inversion Principle
B. Diodic Inversion Principle
C. Dependency Inversion Principle
D. All of the above
E. None of these

Q.12 What is full form of SMPS ?

A. Simple Mode Power Supply
B. Switch Mode Power Supply
C. Storage Mode Power Supply
D. Storage Mode Power Shortage
E. None of these

Q.13 Which of the following is the full form of BCD?

A. Binary Coded Decimal
B. Bit Coded Decimal
C. Binary Coded Digit
D. Bit Coded Digit
E. None of these

Q.14 What is the full form of DEFRAG in the parlance of HDD operations?

A. Defragile
B. Defragmentation
C. Defracture
D. All of the above
E. None of these

Q.15 What does LAN stand for?

A. Local Area Nodes
B. Large Area Network
C. Large Area Nodes
D. Local Area Network
E. None of these

Q.16 What does BIOS stand for?

A. Basic Input Output Software
B. Basic Input Output System
C. Basic Input Output Standards
D. All of the above
E. None of these

Q.17 What does WLAN stand for?
A. Wireless Local Area Network
B. Wide Local Area Network
C. Wind Light Atmospheric Nature
D. Wireless Local Area Node
E. None of these

Q.18 GSM stands for __________.
A. Global System for Mobile Communications
B. Global system map
C. Global system master
D. Global system mode
E. None of these

Q.19 The ALU of a computer responds to the commands coming from ______.
A. Primary memory
B. Control section
C. External memory
D. Cache memory
E. None of these

Q.20 What is the full form of IP?
A. Internal Protocol
B. Internet Protocol
C. Interior Protocol
D. All of the above
E. None of these

Q.21 What is the full form of UTP?
A. Unshielded Twisted Pair
B. Universal Transmission Path
C. User Time Precision
D. Unified Transmission Protocol
E. None of these

Q.22 What does URL stand for?
A. Universal Route Locator
B. Uniform Resource Locator
C. United Road Locator
D. Union Route locator
E. None of these

Q.23 What is the full form of ISP?
A. Internet Service Provider
B. Internet Segregation Principle
C. Informal Segregation Principle
D. Informal Service Provider
E. None of these

Q.24 What is the full form of MAN?
A. Metropolitan Area Network
B. Mobile Area Network
C. Memory Authority Network
D. Metropolitan Authority Network
E. None of these

Q.25 In 'Internet' the term WWWW, the 4th W stands for __________.
A. Worm
B. Web
C. Wreck
D. Word
E. None of these

Q.26 What is the full form of COMPUTER?
A. Compulsory Operated Machine Privately Used for Technology Education and Research
B. Common Operating Machine Purposely Used for Technological and Educational Research
C. Conveniently Operated Method Particularly Used for Technology Education and Research
D. All of the above
E. None of these

Q.27 ASCII stands for ________.
A. American Standard Code for Information Interface
B. American Standard Code for Information Interchange
C. American Standard Code for Interface Interchange
D. American Standard Coder for Information Interchange
E. None of these

Q.28 What does EPROM stand for?
A. Erasable Programmable Read Only Memory
B. Electric Programmable Read Only Memory
C. Editable Programmable Read-Only Memory
D. Evaluable Philotic Random Optic Memory
E. None of these

Q.29 What is the full form of HTTP?
A. Hyper text transfer protocol
B. Hyper text transfer package
C. Hyphenation text program
D. All of the above
E. None of these

Q.30 What does VGA stand for?
A. Video Global Array
B. Visual Graph Array
C. Video Graphics Array
D. All of the above
E. None of these

// Smart Answer Sheet //

| Correct | Percentage of students who answered correctly. | Skipped | Percentage of students who skipped. |

Q.	Ans.	Correct / Skipped	Q.	Ans.	Correct / Skipped	Q.	Ans.	Correct / Skipped	Q.	Ans.	Correct / Skipped	Q.	Ans.	Correct / Skipped	Q.	Ans.	Correct / Skipped
1	B	78.05 % / 13.92 %	6	B	76.39 % / 22.39 %	11	C	12.41 % / 78.99 %	16	B	45.31 % / 45.35 %	21	A	42.73 % / 52.14 %	26	B	76.14 % / 22.61 %
2	B	76.14 % / 15.81 %	7	B	76.55 % / 13.06 %	12	B	53.49 % / 35.05 %	17	A	77.82 % / 17.26 %	22	B	79.99 % / 15.05 %	27	B	89.69 % / 10.29 %
3	A	61.85 % / 30.06 %	8	A	76.5 % / 21.2 %	13	A	54.18 % / 45.11 %	18	A	45.39 % / 50.17 %	23	A	82.61 % / 10.07 %	28	A	69.01 % / 30.22 %
4	A	56.63 % / 42.73 %	9	A	56.42 % / 41.73 %	14	B	48.25 % / 37.52 %	19	B	57.83 % / 36.71 %	24	A	87.84 % / 10.95 %	29	A	76.28 % / 12.01 %
5	B	66.33 % / 31.11 %	10	D	84.67 % / 10.51 %	15	D	87.64 % / 11.41 %	20	B	81.51 % / 17.1 %	25	A	60.83 % / 33.88 %	30	C	44.07 % / 36.3 %

//Hints and Solutions//

1. The central processing unit (CPU) is the unit which performs most of the processing inside a computer. To control instructions and data flow to and from other parts of the computer, the CPU relies heavily on a chipset, which is a group of microchips located on the motherboard.

Hence the correct option is (B).

2. USB (Universal Serial Bus) is the most popular connection used to connect a computer to devices such as digital cameras, printers, scanners, and external hard drives. USB is a cross-platform technology that is supported by most of the major operating systems.

Hence the correct option is (B).

3. EEPROM stands for Electrically Erasable Programmable Read-Only Memory and is a type of non-volatile memory used in computers, integrated into microcontrollers for smart cards and remote keyless systems, and other electronic devices to store relatively small amounts of data but allowing individual bytes to be erased and reprogrammed.

Hence the correct option is (A).

4. UNIVAC (Universal Automatic Computer) is a line of electronic digital stored-program computers starting with the products of the Eckert–Mauchly Computer Corporation.

Hence the correct option is (A).

5. DNS stands for Domain Name System. DNS is system, that allows you to use your web browser to find websites as well as send and receive emails or requests.

Hence the correct option is (B).

6. Wide area network is a telecommunication network or computer network that extends over a large geographical distance/place. Wide area networks are often established with leased telecommunication circuits.

Hence the correct option is (B)

7. VIRUS stands for 'Vital Information Resource Under Seige'. It is a segment of self-replicating code planted illegally in a computer program, often to damage or shut down a system or network.

Hence the correct option is (B).

8. RAM stands for random access memory, a component that allows your computer to store data in short-term for quicker access. Your computer loads the program or document, you request from the storage disk to memory, then accesses each piece of information from the memory.

Hence the correct option is (A).

9. Million Instructions Per Second (MIPS) is a method of measuring the raw speed of a computer's processor, but not the whole system. 1 MIPS is 10,00,000 instructions per second.

Hence the correct option is (A).

10. CD-ROM stands for "Compact Disc Read-Only Memory." A CD-ROM is a CD that can be read by a computer with an optical drive. The "ROM" part of the term means the data on the disc is "read-only," or cannot be altered or erased.

Hence the correct option is (D).

11. In object-oriented design, a dependency inversion principle is a specific form of loosely coupling software modules. When following this principle, the conventional dependency relationships established from high-level, policy-setting modules to low-level, dependency modules are reversed, thus rendering high-level modules independent of the low-level module implementation details.

Hence the correct option is (C).

12. Switch mode power supply (SMPS) is an electronic power supply that incorporates a switching regulator to convert electrical power efficiently.

Hence the correct option is (B).

13. A binary-coded decimal (BCD) is a type of binary representation for decimal values where each digit is represented by a fixed number of binary bits, usually between four and eight.

Hence the correct option is (A).

14. Defragmentation is the process of locating the noncontiguous fragments of data into which a computer file may be divided as it is stored on a hard disk, and rearranging the fragments and restoring them into fewer fragments or into the whole file.

Hence the correct option is (B).

15. LAN stands for local area network. It is a local computer network for communication between computers; especially a network connecting computers and word processors and other electronic office equipment to create a communication system between offices.

Hence the correct option is (D).

16. Basic Input Output System, also known as the System BIOS is non-volatile firmware used to perform hardware initialization during the booting process and to provide runtime services for operating systems and programs.

Hence the correct option is (B).

17. A wireless local area network (WLAN) is a wireless distribution method for two or more devices that use high-frequency radio waves and often include an access point to the Internet.

A WLAN allows users to move around the coverage area, often a home or small office, while maintaining a network connection.

Hence the correct option is (A).

18. GSM (Global System for Mobile communications) is a standard developed by the European Telecommunications Standards Institute to describe the protocols for second-generation (2G) digital cellular networks used by mobile devices such as mobile phones and tablets.

Hence the correct option is (A).

19. The ALU of a computer responds to the commands coming from control section. The control unit is a component of a computer's central processing unit that directs the operation of the processor.

Hence the correct option is (B).

20. IP stands for internet protocol (protocol means set of rules) which means rules for communication over the internet. IP is basically a unique address for your website.

For example:- if you are transferring files over the internet then the internet will use FTP (File transfer protocol), etc.

Hence the correct option is (B).

21. Unshielded twisted pair (UTP) cables are widely used in the computer and telecommunications industry as Ethernet cables and telephone wires. In a UTP cable, conductors which form a single circuit are twisted around each other in order to cancel out electromagnetic interference (EMI) from external sources.

Hence the correct option is (A).

22. URL stands for uniform resource locator. A URL specifies the addresses of various network resources on the Internet.

Hence the correct option is (B).

23. ISP stands for Internet Service Provider which provides Internet connections and services to individuals and organizations. ISPs are responsible for making sure you can access the Internet, routing Internet traffic, resolving domain names, and maintaining the network infrastructure that makes Internet access possible.

Hence the correct option is (A).

24. A metropolitan area network, or MAN, consists of a computer network across an entire city, college campus or a small region. A MAN is larger than a LAN, which is typically limited to a single building or site. It is a computer network that interconnects users with computer resources in a geographic area or region larger than that covered by even a large local area network (LAN) but smaller than the area covered by a wide area network (WAN).

Hence the correct option is (A).

25. World Wide Web Worm (WWWW) was a search engine for the World Wide Web (WWW). It was developed by Oliver McBryan at the University of Colorado located in Boulder, Colorado, United States.

Hence the correct option is (A).

26. COMPUTER stands for Common Operating Machine Purposely Used for Technological and Educational Research. Computer is an electronic device for storing and processing data, typically in binary form, according to instructions given to it in a variable program.

Hence the correct option is (B).

27. ASCII abbreviated from American Standard Code for Information Interchange, is a character encoding standard for electronic communication. ASCII codes represent text in computers, telecommunications equipment, and other devices.

Hence the correct option is (B).

28. EPROM stands for Erasable Programmable Read-Only Memory. EPROM is a read-only memory whose contents can be erased by ultraviolet light or other means and reprogrammed using a pulsed voltage.

Hence the correct option is (A).

29. Hypertext Transfer Protocol is an application-layer protocol used for data communication. It is the base of data communication in the World Wide Web. It provides a standard for web browsers that facilitates users to exchange information over the internet.

Hence the correct option is (A).

30. VGA stands for "Video Graphics Array." It is the standard monitor or display interface used in most PCs. The VGA standard was originally developed by IBM in 1987 and allowed for a display resolution of 640x480 pixels.

Hence the correct option is (C).

Q.1 Which of the following is the first PC virus detected on ARPANET in 1970s?

A. Michelangelo virus   **B.** Brain
C. Creeper   **D.** April first
E. Alien.298

Q.2 Which of the following is a type of virus that consists of self-replicating software that damages files and systems?

A. Viruses   **B.** Trojan horses
C. Bots   **D.** Worms
E. Backdoors

Q.3 Which of the following is a program capable of continually replicating with little or no user intervention?

A. Virus   **B.** Trojan horses
C. Rootkit   **D.** Worms
E. Bots

Q.4 Which of the following is software that, once installed on your computer, tracks your internet browsing habits and sends you popups containing advertisements related to the sites and topics you've visited?

A. Backdoors   **B.** Adware
C. Malware   **D.** Bots
E. Spyware

Q.5 There are _______ types of computer virus.

A. 5   **B.** 7   **C.** 10   **D.** 12
E. 15

Q.6 What is the software called which when get downloaded on a computer scans your hard drive for personal information and your internet browsing habits?

A. Backdoors   **B.** Key-logger
C. Malware   **D.** Antiware
E. Spyware

Q.7 _______ are computer programs that are designed by attackers to gain root or administrative access to your computer.

A. Backdoors   **B.** Rootkits
C. Malware   **D.** Antiware
E. Spyware

Q.8 The attack that focuses on capturing small packets from the network transmitted by other computers and reading the data content in search of any type of information is _______.

A. Phishing   **B.** Eavesdropping
C. Scams   **D.** Exploits
E. Denial of service

Q.9 _______ is the action of recording the keys struck on a keyboard, typically covertly, so that the person using the keyboard is unaware that their actions are being monitored.

A. Denial of service   **B.** Exploits
C. Scams   **D.** Keylogging
E. Spamming

Q.10 _______ is the part of malware such as worms or viruses which performs the malicious action; deleting data, sending spam, or encrypting data.

A. Exploits   **B.** Scams
C. Denial of service   **D.** Payload
E. Spamming

Q.11 What is the route of virus transmission?

A. Moniter   **B.** Flash drive
C. Mouse   **D.** Cable
E. None of these

Q.12 What is the first Boot Sector Virus?

A. Brain   **B.** Elk Cloner
C. Mind   **D.** Creeper
E. Denzuko

Q.13 A computer _______ is a malicious code which self-replicates by copying itself to other programs.

A. Program   **B.** Virus
C. Application   **D.** Worm
E. Trojan

Q.14 Which of them is not an ideal way of spreading the virus?

A. Infected website
B. Emails
C. Official Antivirus CD
D. USB
E. Games

Q.15 In which year Apple II virus came into existence?

A. 1979   **B.** 1980   **C.** 1981   **D.** 1982
E. 1990

Q.16 The virus hides from getting detected by _______ in different ways.

A. 2   **B.** 3   **C.** 4   **D.** 5
E. 1

Q.17 _______ infects the master boot record and it is challenging and a complex task to remove this virus.

A. Boot Sector Virus   **B.** Polymorphic
C. Multipartite   **D.** Trojans
E. None of these

Q.18 _______ gets installed & stays hidden in your computer's memory. It stays involved to the specific type of files which it infects.

A. Boot Sector Virus   **B.** Direct Action Virus
C. Polymorphic Virus   **D.** Multipartite Virus
E. None of these

Q.19 Direct Action Virus is also known as _______.

A. Non-resident virus	**B.** Boot Sector Virus
C. Polymorphic Virus	**D.** Multipartite Virus
E. Space-filler Virus	

Q.20 __________ is also known as cavity virus.

A. Non-resident virus	**B.** Overwrite Virus
C. Polymorphic Virus	**D.** Space-filler Virus
E. Multipartite virus	

Q.21 Which of the below-mentioned reasons do not satisfy the reason why people create a computer virus?

A. Research purpose	**B.** Pranks
C. Identity theft	**D.** Protection
E. Steal data	

Q.22 Code Red is a type of ______.

A. Antivirus Program
B. Photo editing software
C. Computer virus
D. Video editing software
E. None of these

Q.23 Attack in which a user creates a packet that appears to be something else?

A. Smurfing	**B.** Trojan
C. E-mail bombing	**D.** Spoofing
E. None of these	

Q.24 The virus that spread in application software is called as __________.

A. Boot virus	**B.** Macro virus
C. File virus	**D.** Anti virus
E. All of the above	

Q.25 An attack in which the user receives unwanted amount of e-mails:

A. Smurfing	**B.** Denial of service
C. E-mail bombing	**D.** Ping storm
E. Malware	

Q.26 Which among the following is the most common source of Viruses to the hard disk of your computer?

A. Incoming Email	**B.** Outgoing Email
C. CD ROM	**D.** Websites
E. All of the above	

Q.27 __________ deletes all the files that it infects.

A. Non-resident virus	**B.** Overwrite Virus
C. Polymorphic Virus	**D.** Multipartite Virus
E. None of these	

Q.28 __________ are difficult to identify as they keep on changing their type and signature.

A. Non-resident virus	**B.** Boot Sector Virus
C. Polymorphic Virus	**D.** Multipartite Virus
E. Overwrite Virus	

Q.29 __________ infects the executables as well as the boot sectors.

A. Non-resident virus	**B.** Boot Sector Virus

C. Polymorphic Virus	**D.** Multipartite Virus
E. Space-filler Virus	

Q.30 __________ Viruses are often transmitted by a floppy disk left in the floppy drive.

A. Trojan Horse	**B.** Boot sector
C. Script	**D.** Logic bomb
E. None of these	

// Smart Answer Sheet //

Correct Percentage of students who answered correctly. **Skipped** Percentage of students who skipped.

Q.	Ans.	Correct / Skipped	Q.	Ans.	Correct / Skipped	Q.	Ans.	Correct / Skipped	Q.	Ans.	Correct / Skipped	Q.	Ans.	Correct / Skipped	Q.	Ans.	Correct / Skipped	Q.	Ans.	Correct / Skipped
1	C	67.44 % / 30.32 %	6	E	46.92 % / 44.32 %	11	B	61.31 % / 32.43 %	16	B	53.51 % / 42.63 %	21	D	81.72 % / 12.05 %	26	A	64.3 % / 32.86 %
2	D	42.56 % / 48.33 %	7	B	40.36 % / 38.59 %	12	B	77.95 % / 18.39 %	17	A	87.18 % / 11.96 %	22	C	79.45 % / 18.85 %	27	B	78.14 % / 11.62 %
3	A	57.68 % / 39.67 %	8	B	40.11 % / 38.18 %	13	B	82.6 % / 16.27 %	18	B	65.35 % / 32.43 %	23	D	52.33 % / 39.84 %	28	C	82.46 % / 11.46 %
4	B	49.8 % / 38.91 %	9	D	67.64 % / 31.86 %	14	C	54.74 % / 42.94 %	19	A	80.37 % / 17.78 %	24	B	78.0 % / 19.69 %	29	D	64.68 % / 30.2 %
5	C	66.49 % / 32.52 %	10	D	57.5 % / 34.91 %	15	C	43.94 % / 32.04 %	20	D	88.91 % / 10.37 %	25	C	53.61 % / 34.49 %	30	B	59.94 % / 37.73 %

//Hints and Solutions//

1. The Creeper virus was first detected on ARPANET, the forerunner of the Internet, in the early 1970s. Creeper used the ARPANET to infect DEC PDP-10 computers running the TENEX operating system. Creeper gained access via the ARPANET and copied itself to the remote system where the message, "I'm the creeper, catch me if you can!" was displayed. The Reaper program was created to delete Creeper.

Hence, the correct option is (C).

2. A worm is a type of virus that spreads through your computer by creating duplicates of itself on other drives, systems, and networks. Computer worms replicate functional copies of themselves and can cause the same type of damage. In contrast to viruses, which require the spreading of an infected host file, worms are standalone software and do not require a host program or human help to propagate(Self-Replicate).

Hence, the correct option is (D).

3. Virus is a program capable of continually replicating with little or no user intervention. A computer virus is a malicious piece of computer code designed to spread from device to device. A subset of malware, these self-copying threats are usually designed to damage a device or steal data.

Hence, the correct option is (A).

4. Adware is software that displays unwanted (and sometimes irritating) pop-up adverts which can appear on your computer or mobile device. Some adware has keyloggers and spyware built into the program, leading to greater damage to your computer and possible invasion of your private data.

Hence, the correct option is (B).

5. There are a total of 10 types of virus. These are categorized based on their working and characteristics. These are-

1. System or Boot Sector Virus
2. Direct Action Virus
3. Resident Virus
4. Multipartite Virus
5. Polymorphic Virus
6. Overwrite Virus
7. Space-filler Virus
8. File infectors
9. Macro Virus
10. Rootkit virus.

Hence, the correct option is (C).

6. Spyware is a malicious computer program that does exactly what its name implies-i.e., spies on you. After downloading itself onto your computer either through an email you opened, a website you visited, or a program you downloaded, spyware scans your hard drive for personal information and your internet browsing habits. Some spyware programs contain keyloggers that will record personal data you enter into websites, such as

your login usernames and passwords, email addresses, browsing history, online buying habits, etc.

Hence, the correct option is (E).

7. Rootkits are computer programs that are designed by attackers to gain root or administrative access to your computer. Once an attacker gains admin privilege, it becomes a cakewalk for him to exploit your system.

Unlike most viruses, it is not directly destructive and unlike worms, its objective is not to spread infection as wide as possible.

Hence, the correct option is (B).

8. Network eavesdropping is a network layer attack that focuses on capturing small packets from the network transmitted by other computers and reading the data content in search of any type of information.

This type of network attack is generally one of the most effective as a lack of encryption services is used. It is also linked to the collection of metadata.

Hence, the correct option is (B).

9. Keystroke logging often referred to as keylogging or keyboard capturing, is the action of recording (logging) the keys struck on a keyboard, typically covertly, so that the person using the keyboard is unaware that their actions are being monitored. Data can then be retrieved by the person operating the logging program. A keystroke, recorder or keylogger can be either software or hardware.

Hence, the correct option is (D).

10. In computer security, the payload is the part of malware such as worms or viruses which perform the malicious action; deleting data, sending spam, or encrypting data. In addition to the payload, such malware also typically has overhead code aimed at simply spreading itself, or avoiding detection.

Hence, the correct option is (D).

11. The route of virus transmission is the flash drive. Computer viruses usually spread through one of the following:

- Connecting your device to an infected external Flash drive, hard drive or network drive.
- Downloading infected files as email attachments from websites or through file-sharing activities.
- Clicking on links to malicious websites in email, messaging apps or social network posts.
- By visiting compromised websites, aka drive-by downloads, viruses can hide in the HTML thus be downloaded when the webpage loads in your browser.

Hence, the correct option is (B).

12. Richard Skrenta created the first boot sector virus, called Elk Cloner, in 1981. They infect a computer when it boots up or when it accesses the infected floppy disk in the floppy drive. i.e. Once a system is infected with a boot-sector virus, any non-write-protected disk accessed by this system will become infected.

Hence, the correct option is (B).

13. A computer virus is a malicious code which self-replicates by copying itself to other programs. The computer virus gets spread by itself into other executable code or documents. The intention of creating a virus is to infect vulnerable systems.

Hence, the correct option is (B).

14. Official Antivirus CD are not an ideal way of spreading the virus. The ideal means of spreading computer virus are through emails, USB drives that are used portable and injected and ejected in different systems as well as from infected websites. Antivirus selling vendors do not place a virus in their CD and DVD.

Hence, the correct option is (C).

15. In mid-1981, the 1st virus for Apple computers with the name Apple II came into existence. It was also called Elk Cloner, which resided in the boot sectors of a 3.3 floppy disk.

Hence, the correct option is (C).

16. The virus hides from getting detected in 3 different ways. These are by encrypting itself, by altering the disk directory with additional virus bytes or it uses a stealth algorithm to redirect disk data.

Hence, the correct option is (B).

17. Boot Sector Virus infects the master boot record & it is a challenging & complex task to remove such virus. Mostly such virus spreads through removable devices.

Hence, the correct option is (A).

18. Direct Action Virus gets installed & stays hidden in your computer's memory. Such type of virus stays involved in the specific type of files which it infects. A direct action virus is a type of file infector virus that works by attaching itself to an .exe or .com file when installed or executed. Once this occurs, the virus can spread to other existing files and can render them inaccessible.

Hence, the correct option is (B).

19. Direct Action Virus is also known as a non-resident virus that gets installed & stays hidden in your computer's memory. Such type of virus stays involved in the specific type of files which it infects.

Hence, the correct option is (A).

20. Space-filler Virus is also known as cavity virus. Space-filler virus is a rare type of computer virus that try installing itself by filling in empty sections of a file. By only using empty sections of a file, the virus can infect a file without the size of the file changing, making it more difficult to detect.

Hence, the correct option is (D).

21. A computer virus is not created for protection. Virus writers may have other reasons like research purposes, pranks, vandalism, financial gain, identity theft, steal data and some other malicious purposes.

Hence, the correct option is (D).

22. Code Red is a type of Computer virus that was first discovered on 15 July in 2001 as it attacks the servers of Microsoft. It attacked computers running Microsoft's IIS web server. It was the first large scale, mixed threat attack to successfully target enterprise networks. Although the worm had been released on July 13, the largest group of infected computers was seen on July 19, 2001. On that day, the number of infected hosts reached 359,000.

Hence, the correct option is (C).

23. A spoofing attack occurs when a user creates a packet that appears to be something or someone else.

In the context of information security, and especially network security, a spoofing attack is a situation in which a person or program successfully identifies as another by falsifying data, to gain an illegitimate advantage.

Hence, the correct option is (D).

24. A macro virus is a computer virus written in the same macro language used for software programs, including Microsoft Excel or word processors such as Microsoft Word. When a macro virus infects a software application, it causes a sequence of actions to begin automatically when the application is opened.

Hence, the correct option is (B).

25. An email bombing is a form of Internet abuse that is perpetrated through the sending of massive volumes of email to a specific email address with the goal of overflowing the mailbox and overwhelming the mail server hosting the address, making it into some form of denial of service attack. In the case of denial of e-mail bombing, a user sends an excessive amount of unwanted e-mail to someone.

Hence, the correct option is (C).

26. Incoming emails is the most common source of Viruses to the hard disk of a computer. Hackers are using e mail for attacking a computer. The incoming email is the most vulnerable way. In incoming email, virus consists of malicious code that is distributed in email messages, and it can be activated when a user clicks on a link in an email message, opens an email attachment or interacts in some other way with the infected email message.

Hence, the correct option is (A).

27. Overwrite virus deletes all files that it infects. After infecting a system, an overwrite virus begins overwriting files with its own code. These viruses can target specific files or applications or systematically overwrite all files on an infected device. It can be removed by only deleting those infected files. Mostly, it gets spread via emails.

Hence, the correct option is (B).

28. Polymorphic Virus is difficult to identify as they keep on changing their type and signature. They're not easily detectable by traditional antivirus. It usually changes the signature pattern whenever it replicates itself.

Hence, the correct option is (C).

29. A multipartite virus is a fast-moving virus that uses file infectors or boot infectors to attack the boot sector and executable files simultaneously. It infects the computer or get into any system through multiple mediums and are hard to remove. Most viruses either affect the boot sector, the system or the program files.

Hence, the correct option is (D).

30. Boot sector Viruses are often transmitted by a floppy disk left in the floppy drive.

A boot sector virus is a type of virus that infects the boot sector of floppy disks or the Master Boot Record (MBR) of hard disks (some infect the boot sector of the hard disk instead of the MBR). While boot sector viruses infect at a BIOS level, they use DOS commands to spread to other floppy disks.

The boot sector is the first software loaded onto your computer. An example of a boot sector virus is Parity Boot. This virus's payload displays the message PARITY CHECK and freezes the operating system, rendering the computer useless.

 A boot sector is a region of a hard disk, floppy disk, optical disc, or other data storage device that contains machine code to be loaded into random-access memory (RAM) by a computer system's built-in firmware.

Hence, the correct option is (B).

Q.1 You can copy data or formulas ____________.
A. With the copy, paste and cut commands on the edit menu
B. With commands on a shortcut menu
C. With buttons on the standard toolbar
D. (A), (B) and (C)
E. None of these

Q.2 What is the intersection of a row and a column called?
A. Form
B. Cursor
C. Cell
D. Record
E. None of these

Q.3 Which command brings you to the first slide in your presentation?
A. Next slide button
B. Page up
C. Ctrl + Home
D. Ctrl + End
E. Ctrl + Enter

Q.4 Microsoft word is an example of which of the following?
A. Application software
B. System software
C. Open source software
D. Software useful to run computer system
E. None of the above

Q.5 In MS-office XP, "Ruler" for top and the left margin is available in which menu?
A. Insert
B. Review
C. View
D. Home
E. None of the above

Q.6 Microsoft Front page is a pack of MS Office, it is useful to make which of the following?
A. Web Pages
B. Application Programs
C. Files
D. Spreadsheet files
E. None of these

Q.7 Which key is used to indent a paragraph in MS-Word?
A. Alt
B. Tab
C. Ctrl
D. Esc
E. Home

Q.8 To return the remainder after a number is divided by a divisor in EXCEL we use ________ function.
A. ROUND( )
B. FACT( )
C. MOD( )
D. DIV( )
E. None of these

Q.9 How can you link Excel worksheet data to a Word document?
A. One can link with the right drag method.
B. One can link with the hyperlink.
C. One can link with the copy and paste special commands.
D. Both (A) and (B)

E. None of these

Q.10 What is name the function in Ms-Excel to count a number of cells?
A. COUNTIF
B. DIVIF
C. SUNIF
D. AVERAGE
E. None of the above

Q.11 What are the columns in a Microsoft Access table called?
A. Rows
B. Records
C. Fields
D. Columns
E. Cell

Q.12 To start Microsoft PowerPoint application in Windows 2007, we press ________.
A. Click on Start >> Programs >> All Programs >> Microsoft PowerPoint
B. Hit Ctrl + C then type ppoint.exe and Enter
C. Click Start >> All Programs >> Microsoft Office >> PowerPoint
D. Either (A) or (B)
E. None of the above

Q.13 What happens when you click on Insert >> Picture >> Clip Art in MS word 2003?
A. It inserts a clipart picture into the document.
B. It lets you choose clipart to insert into the document.
C. It opens the Clip Art taskbar.
D. Both (A) and (B)
E. None of the above

Q.14 In PowerPoint Ellipse, Motion is a predefined as ________.
A. Animation Scheme
B. Design Template
C. Color Scheme
D. Both (B) and (C)
E. None of these

Q.15 Text boundary can be displayed or hidden from-
A. Customize from Tools menu
B. Auto text option from Insert menu
C. Options from Tools menu
D. Outline from View menu
E. None of the above

Q.16 A worksheet can have a maximum of ________ number of rows in Excel 2003.
A. 256
B. 1024
C. 32000
D. 65536
E. 38835

Q.17 What function displays row data in a column or column data in a row?
A. Hyperlink
B. Index
C. Transpose
D. Rows
E. Cells

Q.18 To undo the last work, we press ________.
A. Ctrl+U
B. Ctrl+Y

C. Ctrl+Z
D. Ctrl+W
E. None of these

Q.19 In which menu 'drop cap' option is found in MS Word 2007?
A. Home
B. Insert
C. Review
D. Reference
E. Enter

Q.20 Which of the following is a graphics solution for Word Processors?
A. Paint
B. WordArt
C. Drop Cap
D. Clipart
E. None of these

Q.21 On an excel sheet, the active cell is indicated by which of the following?
A. Red border
B. Dotted border
C. Blinking border
D. Dark wide border
E. None of the above

Q.22 Which of the following is not a document view?
A. Draft
B. Work View
C. Web Layout view
D. Print Layout view
E. None of these

Q.23 How can we set vertical alignment?
A. Page Setup command from File menu
B. Page Setup command from Format menu
C. Paragraph command from Format menu
D. Font command from Format menu
E. None of the above

Q.24 In MS Word, by default, setting of Line spacing is
__________.

A. 1
B. 1.15
C. 1.5
D. 2
E. 2.5

Q.25 To view all PowerPoint slides together we select

__________.

A. Slide Sorter View
B. Slide Merger View
C. Slide Vary View
D. Either (B) or (C)
E. None of the above

Q.26 Which of the following menus has a background in PowerPoint 2003?
A. Format
B. View
C. Insert
D. Slide show
E. None of these

Q.27 What is the maximum number of columns in a worksheet of Excel 2007?
A. 1024
B. 2048
C. 256
D. 3072
E. None of these

Q.28 Which language does MS-Word use to create Macros?
A. Visual C++
B. Visual Basic
C. FoxPro
D. Access
E. None of these

Q.29 How will MS Word respond in a repeated word?
A. A Red wavy line under the repeated word
B. A Green wavy line under the repeated word
C. A Blue wavy line under the repeated word
D. Both (A) and (B)
E. None of the above

Q.30 Which of the following is an example of Automatic Text formatting?
A. Underlining Hyperlink
B. Adjusting extra space
C. Replacing two hyphens with a hyphen
D. (A), (B) and (C)
E. None of these

// Smart Answer Sheet //

Correct Percentage of students who answered correctly.   **Skipped** Percentage of students who skipped.

Q.	Ans.	Correct / Skipped	Q.	Ans.	Correct / Skipped	Q.	Ans.	Correct / Skipped	Q.	Ans.	Correct / Skipped	Q.	Ans.	Correct / Skipped	Q.	Ans.	Correct / Skipped
1	D	86.54 % / 12.47 %	6	A	69.68 % / 30.21 %	11	C	86.59 % / 12.18 %	16	D	50.11 % / 32.12 %	21	D	85.15 % / 13.86 %	26	A	86.33 % / 12.14 %
2	C	56.61 % / 31.43 %	7	B	48.11 % / 34.95 %	12	C	83.81 % / 13.19 %	17	C	62.0 % / 30.87 %	22	B	64.0 % / 35.42 %	27	E	44.28 % / 34.16 %
3	C	86.06 % / 13.69 %	8	C	45.08 % / 53.92 %	13	C	52.46 % / 47.23 %	18	C	86.45 % / 13.02 %	23	A	66.29 % / 32.61 %	28	B	85.04 % / 13.68 %
4	A	88.02 % / 11.68 %	9	C	69.21 % / 30.17 %	14	A	46.24 % / 31.01 %	19	B	87.01 % / 10.91 %	24	B	57.49 % / 37.62 %	29	A	80.86 % / 10.11 %
5	C	64.19 % / 30.95 %	10	A	61.78 % / 34.3 %	15	C	60.17 % / 31.82 %	20	D	80.75 % / 13.96 %	25	A	88.89 % / 10.52 %	30	D	83.37 % / 13.28 %

//Hints and Solutions//

1. You can copy data or formulas by using the copy, paste, and cut commands on the edit menu, with commands on a shortcut menu, and with buttons on the standard toolbar.

Hence, the correct option is (D).

2. A cell is an intersection of a column and row. Each cell has a unique cell address for example C4 is the cell of Cth row and 4th column. The heavy border around the selected cell is called the cell pointer.

Hence, the correct option is (C).

3. Ctrl + Home command will bring you to the first slide in your presentation. And Ctrl + End command will bring you to the last slide in your presentation.

Hence, the correct option is (C).

4. MS Word is an example of application software developed by the company Microsoft.

- It allows users to type and save documents.
- It is helpful too for making documents.
- It is originally developed by Charles Simonyi and Richard Brodie, it was first released in 1983.
- It is available for Microsoft Windows, Apple OS.

Hence, the correct option is (A).

5. In MS-office XP, "Ruler" for top and the left margin is available in "View" menu.

With Classic Menu for Word 2007/2010/2013/2016/2019 installed, you can click the "View" menu and then choose Ruler in the drop-down menu, and then one may see the horizontal and vertical ruler appearing in the document.

Hence, the correct option is (C).

6. Microsoft Front page is a pack of MS Office, it is useful to make Web Pages.

Microsoft FrontPage(full name Microsoft Office FrontPage) is a discontinued WYSIWYG HTML editor and website administration tool from Microsoft for the Microsoft Windows line of operating systems. It was branded as part of the Microsoft Office suite from 1997 to 2003.

Hence, the correct option is (A).

7. "Tab" key is used to indent a paragraph in MS-Word

To indent the first line of a paragraph, put your cursor at the beginning of the paragraph and press the "tab" key. When you press enter to start the next paragraph, its first line will be indented.

Hence, the correct option is (B).

8. To return the remainder after a number is divided by a divisor in EXCEL we use MOD() function.

The Excel MOD() function returns the remainder of two numbers after division. For example, MOD(16,3) = 1. The result of MOD() carries the same sign as the divisor. Use the MOD() function to get a remainder after division.

Hence, the correct option is (C).

9. You can link Excel worksheet data to a Word document with the copy and paste special commands. And linking of an Excel file to a Word document is the best way to import data. It ensures that the Word document is updated every time the data in the Excel file changes.

Hence, the correct option is (C).

10. The COUNTIF function is used in Ms-Excel to count a number of cells.

Excel contains several functions to help you count the number of cells in a range that are blank or contain certain types of data. COUNTIF is used to count cells that meet specified criteria.

Hence, the correct option is (A).

11. The columns in a Microsoft Access table are called Fields.

A Table is very much like a data table or spreadsheet containing records (i.e., rows) arranged in different fields (i.e., columns). In Access, columns are referred to as fields. When you organize your data by entering it into different fields, you are organizing it by type. Each field contains one type of data.

Hence, the correct option is (C).

12. To start the Microsoft PowerPoint application in Windows 2007, we first press "start" button, then the "All Programs" option is selected. In "All Program", one will find "Microsoft Office" by clicking it, one will find "PowerPoint".

Hence, the correct option is (C).

13. When we click on "Insert" then a pop-up window will open search and click on "Picture" then go to Clip Art and click. The Clip Art taskbar is being opened, in MS word 2003. The Clip art taskbar is used to customize the clip arts.

Hence, the correct option is (C).

14. In PowerPoint Ellipse, Motion is predefined as an animation scheme.

In PowerPoint Ellipse, An animation scheme is just a predefined slide transition and a collection of animatic effects applied to slide objects. One of the most basic types of animation schemes is "Appear". This just defines the paragraphs of text to appear one at a time. An animation effect is a special visual or sound effect added to a text or an object on a slide or chart.

Hence, the correct option is (A).

15. "Text boundaries" checked in Word's Options, however, the cell boundaries will still be outlined with a dotted line in Print Layout and Web Layout views.

Find this setting on the View tab of Tools > Options in Word 2003 and earlier versions.

In Word 2007 and higher versions, it is under Show document content on the Advanced tab of Office/File > Options > Advanced.

Hence, the correct option is (C).

16. The worksheet of Excel 2003 is made up of 65,536 rows and 256 columns. Each row and column is called a division cell and the data is stored here.

Hence, the correct option is (D).

17. Transpose function displays row data in a column or column data in a row.

Transpose, just, rotates the table (data area) of the worksheet to convert rows into columns and columns into rows. This function will convert a horizontal range of cells into a vertical and vertical range of cells into a horizontal.

Hence, the correct option is (C).

18. To undo the last work, we press Ctrl + Z. Ctrl + U is used to underline text. Ctrl + W is used to close a word document. And Ctrl + Y is used to redo an action previously undone or repeat an action.

Hence, the correct option is (C).

19. In the "Insert" menu 'drop cap' option is found in MS Word 2007.

Open a word document in Word 2010 or 2007, and select the letter you want to insert as 'drop cap'.

Click on the "Insert" tab, and in the "Text" group you willget the "Drop Cap" button.

Hence, the correct option is (B).

20. Clipart is a graphics solution for Word Processors.

Clip art refers to a graphic or a picture that you can insert in your document. It comes in different formats and styles. It is used to enhance the appearance of a document. Clip art is a collection of pictures or images that can be imported into a document or another program.

Hence, the correct option is (D).

21. On an excel sheet, the active cell is indicated by a dark wide border.

Neither a dotted border or a blinking border is used to identify the active cell in an excel worksheet because both can't highlight any cell as the dark wide border does. Here, the active cell is identified by a dark outline surrounding the wall. One can see the Active Cell name in the "Name Box" on the top left hand of the Excel sheet.

Hence, the correct option is (D).

22. Work View is not a document view but Print Layout, Web Layout, Outline, Draft all are document view.

The document view buttons appear in the lower-right corner of the application. They also appear on the "View" tab of the Ribbon in the "Views" button group and the "Immersive" button group. Clicking any of these buttons changes the working view of your document. You can then switch to a different view by clicking another view button.

Hence, the correct option is (B).

23. We set vertical alignment as follows:

First, we will choose Page Setup from the File menu. Then, we will click the Layout tab. In the Page Setup section, click the Vertical Alignment dropdown and choose Center.

Hence, the correct option is (A).

24. The default line spacing in MS Word is 1.15. By default, paragraphs are followed by a blank line and headings have a space above them. Go to Home > Line and Paragraph Spacing. Select Line Spacing Options, and then choose the options you want under Spacing.

Hence, the correct option is (B).

25. To view all PowerPoint slides together we select "Slide Sorter View".

In Slide Sorter view, one can select one slide, two or more slides that are next to each other, or two or more slides that are not next to each other. To view all slides together, click on the first slide, press and hold the "Shift" key, and then click on the last slide.

Hence, the correct option is (A).

26. "Format" has a background in PowerPoint 2003.

In PowerPoint 2003, we can easily add and design background in our presentation from the "Format" drop-down menu. However, in PowerPoint 2007, 2010, 2013, 2016, and 2019, the Format menu disappeared, and we can't design, customize, and apply background from there any longer.

Hence, the correct option is (A).

27. If you are working on Excel 2007 or any of the latest versions, then, there are 1048576 rows and 16384 columns. The last column, in this case, is XFD. And the last row is 1048576. If you are working on Excel 2003, then, there are 65536 rows and 256 columns.

Hence, the correct option is (E).

28. MS-Word uses Visual Basic language to create Macros. Visual Basic is a third-generation event-driven programming language from Microsoft for its Component Object Model (COM) programming.

Hence, the correct option is (B).

29. MS Word will represent a red wavy line under the repeated word. A Green wavy line comes whenever you have a grammar mistake.

Hence, the correct option is (A).

30. Automatic text formatting means that the text keeps on getting formatted automatically while we are typing the text into a Writer document. Such as underlining hyperlinks, adjusting the extra space, and replacing two hyphens with a hyphen.

Hence, the correct option is (D).

Q.1 These devices provide a means of communication between a computer and outer world:

A. I/O   **B.** Storage   **C.** Compact   **D.** Drivers
E. Memory

Q.2 Identify the blank space in the diagram.

Input data → Input Device → Input data in coded form → ______ → Processed Data → Output device → Result →

A. Processor   **B.** Memory
C. CPU   **D.** Storage
E. None of these

Q.3 What does GUI stand for?

A.   Graphical User Instruction
B.   Ground User Interface
C.   General User Instruction
D.   Graphical User Interface
E.   none of these

Q.4 Which of the following is not a point-and-draw device?

A. Keypad   **B.** Trackball
C. Touch screen   **D.** Mouse
E. Storage

Q.5 A device used for video games, flight simulators, training simulators and for controlling industrial robots.

A. Mouse   **B.** Light pen
C. Joystick   **D.** Keyboard
E. None of these

Q.6 Which are the input devices that enable direct data entry into a computer system from source documents?

A.   Data Scanning devices
B.   Data retrieving devices
C.   Data acquiring devices
D.   System Access devices
E.   None of these

Q.7 Which of the following is a type of image scanner?

A. Flat-held   **B.** Hand-led
C. Flat-bed   **D.** Compact
E. None of these

Q.8 Which of the following is capable of recognizing a pre-specified type of mark by pencil or pen?

A. OMR   **B.** Winchester
C. Bar code reader   **D.** Image Scanner
E. None of these

Q.9 Input Devices that use a special ink that contains magnetizable particles of iron oxide are ______.

A. Optical disks   **B.** Magnetic disks
C. MICR   **D.** Magnetic drives

E. None of these

Q.10 A printer that prints one line at a time and has a predefined set of characters is called ______.

A. Laser   **B.** Drum
C. Inkjet   **D.** Impact
E. None of these

Q.11 Which of the following is the name of the plotter as well as a printer?

A. Flatbed   **B.** Laser
C. Drum   **D.** Impact
E. None of these

Q.12 Name the device that converts text information into spoken sentences-

A.   Speech Sensors
B.   Compact convertors
C.   Speech Synthesizers
D.   Voice systems
E.   None of these

Q.13 Which of the following is a temporary output?

A. Hard copy   **B.** Soft copy
C. Duplicate copy   **D.** On paper
E. None of these

Q.14 In MICR, C stands for-

A. code   **B.** colour
C. computer   **D.** character
E. None of these

Q.15 The joystick is a _________ stick that moves the graphic cursor in the direction the stick is moved.

A. Parallel   **B.** Horizontal
C. Straight   **D.** Vertical
E. None of these

Q.16 The __________ pen is a small input device used to select and display objects on a screen.

A. Ink   **B.** Magnetic
C. Light   **D.** Joystick
E. None of the above

Q.17 A device for converting handwritten impressions into coded characters & positional coordinates for input to a computer is-

A. Touch panel   **B.** Mouse
C. Wand   **D.** Writing tablet
E. None of these

Q.18 Which device of computer operation dispenses with the use of the keyboard?

A. Joystick   **B.** Mouse
C. Light pen   **D.** Touch

Q.19 _______ keys are present on the top row of the keyboard.

A. Function
B. Type writer
C. Numeric
D. Navigation
E. None of these

Q.20 Dot-matrix, Deskjet, Inkjet and Laser are all types of which computer peripherals?

A. Printers
B. Software
C. Monitors
D. Keyboards
E. None of these

Q.21 Which among the device that converts computer output into a form that can be transmitted over a telephone line?

A. Teleport
B. Multiplexer
C. Concentrator
D. Modem
E. None of these

Q.22 A light-sensitive device that converts drawing, printed text or other images into digital form is-

A. Keyboard
B. Plotter
C. Scanner
D. OMR
E. None of these

Q.23 What type of devices are computer speakers or headphones?

A. Input
B. Input/Output
C. Software
D. Output
E. None of these

Q.24 Laser printers belong to-

A. line printer
B. page printer
C. band printer
D. dot matrix printer
E. None of these

Q.25 Joysticks typically have a button on _______that is used to select the option pointed by the cursor.

A. Bottom
B. Left
C. Right
D. Top
E. None of these

Q.26 Which output device of a computer is used for training presentations?

A. Plotters
B. Multimedia projectors
C. Computer monitor
D. Inject or laser printer
E. None of these

Q.27 The wheel located between the two standard buttons on a mouse is used to _______.

A. Click on web pages
B. Shutdown
C. Click and select items
D. Scroll
E. None of the above

Q.28 The _______ may also be called the screen or monitor.

A. Printer
B. Scanner
C. Hard disk
D. Display

E. None of these

Q.29 A joystick is primarily used to/for-

A. control sound on the screen
B. computer gaming
C. enter text
D. draw pictures
E. None of these

Q.30 Which of the following groups consists of only input devices?

A. Mouse, Keyboard, Monitor
B. Mouse, Keyboard, Printer
C. Mouse, Keyboard, Plotter
D. Mouse, Keyboard, Scanner
E. None of these

// Smart Answer Sheet //

| Correct | Percentage of students who answered correctly. | Skipped | Percentage of students who skipped. |

Q.	Ans.	Correct / Skipped	Q.	Ans.	Correct / Skipped	Q.	Ans.	Correct / Skipped	Q.	Ans.	Correct / Skipped	Q.	Ans.	Correct / Skipped	Q.	Ans.	Correct / Skipped
1	A	80.93 % / 14.52 %	6	A	45.73 % / 33.97 %	11	C	67.36 % / 32.64 %	16	C	42.91 % / 51.42 %	21	D	67.09 % / 30.92 %	26	B	48.04 % / 48.09 %
2	C	78.37 % / 18.11 %	7	C	45.09 % / 43.95 %	12	C	46.94 % / 45.97 %	17	D	62.75 % / 30.28 %	22	C	54.94 % / 30.8 %	27	D	80.89 % / 14.6 %
3	D	45.72 % / 30.31 %	8	A	61.67 % / 32.57 %	13	B	48.45 % / 44.46 %	18	B	42.93 % / 50.55 %	23	D	67.18 % / 30.93 %	28	D	77.26 % / 14.06 %
4	A	54.54 % / 44.07 %	9	C	49.66 % / 40.13 %	14	D	47.95 % / 50.02 %	19	A	67.64 % / 30.53 %	24	B	44.61 % / 53.77 %	29	B	88.55 % / 11.1 %
5	C	41.78 % / 53.66 %	10	B	40.21 % / 57.01 %	15	D	66.31 % / 30.23 %	20	A	42.84 % / 38.62 %	25	D	47.25 % / 45.39 %	30	D	81.32 % / 17.7 %

//Hints and Solutions//

1. The I/O i.e. the input/output devices provide a means of communication between the computer and the outer world. They are often referred to as peripheral devices sometimes. For example, Keyboard, mouse, printer, speaker and scanner etc.

Hence, the correct option is (A).

2. Firstly, the input is given to the input device, then the data is coded in internal form and is sent to the CPU. Further, the processed data is sent to the output device and the result is obtained.

Hence, the correct option is (C).

3. GUI stands for a graphical user interface. A graphical user interface basically provides a set of graphical elements on the screen to the users. Commonly used for point-and-draw devices.

Hence, the correct option is (D).

4. All except the keypad are point-and-draw devices. They are used to rapidly point to and select a graphic icon or menu item from multiple options displayed on the GUI of a screen.

Hence, the correct option is (A).

5. Joystick is the device used for the same. It is a point-and-draw device. It has a click button, a stick, a ball, a socket as well as a light indicator.

Hence, the correct option is (C).

6. Data scanning devices are the input devices that enable direct data entry into a computer system from source documents. They eliminate the need to key in text data into the computer. It demands the high quality of input documents.

Hence, the correct option is (A).

7. Flat-bed is a type of image scanner. Image scanners are the input devices that translate paper documents into an electronic format for storage in a computer. Stored images can be altered or manipulated with image-processing software.

Hence, the correct option is (C).

8. OMR is capable of recognizing a pre-specified type of mark by pencil or pen. OMR stands for optical mark reader. It is the process of capturing human-marked data from document forms such as surveys and tests. They are used to read questionnaires, multiple choice examination paper in the form of shaded areas.

Hence, the correct option is (A).

9. Input Devices that use a special ink that contains magnetizable particles of iron oxide are MICR. MICR stands for Magnetic-Ink-Character Recognition. MICR is a technology used primarily to identify and process checks. The MICR on a check is the string of characters that appears at the bottom left of the check. It consists of three groups of numbers, including the bank routing number, the account number, and the check number.

Hence, the correct option is (C).

10. A printer that prints one line at a time and has a predefined set of characters is called drum printers. They have a cylindrical drum with characters embossed on its surface in the form of circular bands.

Hence, the correct option is (B).

11. The drum is the name of a plotter as well as a printer. Drum printers have a predefined set of characters and print one line at a time. Drum plotters is an ideal device for architects and others who need to generate high-precision hard copy graphics output of widely varying sizes.

Hence, the correct option is (C).

12. A speech synthesizer converts text information into spoken sentences. It is used for reading out text information to blind people. Allowing people to communicate effectively.

Hence, the correct option is (C).

13. Soft copy is a temporary output. A soft copy is an electronic copy of some type of data, such as a file viewed on a computer's display or transmitted as an e-mail attachment. Such material, when printed, is referred to as a hard copy. A soft copy is a digital reproduction of a physical document. For example, if you scanned a tax form into your computer, you would be creating a soft copy of it. The most common method of displaying a soft copy uses a computer monitor or another display, such as a smartphone screen.

Hence, the correct option is (B).

14. The full form of MICR is magnetic ink character recognition. So, in MICR, C stands for character. MICR code is a character-recognition technology used mainly by the banking industry to ease the processing and clearance of cheques and other documents. The technology allows MICR readers to scan and read the information directly into a data-collection device.

Hence, the correct option is (D).

15. The joystick is a lever that moves in all directions and controls the movement of a pointer or some other display symbol. A joystick is similar to a mouse, except that with a mouse the cursor stops moving as soon as you stop moving the mouse.

Hence, the correct option is (D).

16. The Light pen is a small input device used to select and display objects on a screen. A light pen is a computer input device in the form of a light-sensitive wand used in conjunction with a computer's cathode-ray tube (CRT) display. It allows the user to point to displayed objects or draw on the screen in a similar way to a touchscreen but with greater positional accuracy.

Hence, the correct option is (C).

17. A device for converting handwritten impressions into coded characters & positional coordinates for input to a computer is a Writing tablet. A tablet is a type of notebook computer that has an LCD screen on which the user can write using finger and swipe actions or by using a special-purpose pen, or stylus. All user input is directly via the LCD screen and not a keyboard or mouse. On a tablet computer, handwriting is digitized and can be converted to standard text through handwriting recognition, or it can remain as handwritten text. The stylus also can be used to type on a pen-based key layout where the lettered keys are arranged differently

than a QWERTY keyboard. Tablet PCs can be equipped with a keyboard and/or a mouse for input.

Hence, the correct option is (D).

18. Mouse is an input device, the actual name of which is pointing device, it is mainly used to select items on the computer screen, move towards them and open and close them. The user gives instructions to the computer through the mouse.

Examples of input devices include keyboard, mouse, scanner, digital camera and joystick.

Hence, the correct option is (B).

19. The function keys, also called the F-keys or Fn keys, are located in the top row of nearly all computer keyboards. They typically contain at least F1 through F12 but may include to F16 on some keyboards.

Hence, the correct option is (A).

20. Dot-matrix, Deskjet, Inkjet and Laser are all types of Printers computer peripherals. A computer printer is considered a peripheral, which means it's not a required device. Many people use a computer every day without a printer. However, if the time comes when they need to print something, they'll have to visit somewhere with a printer.

Hence, the correct option is (A).

21. A modem (modulator-demodulator) is a network hardware device that modulates one or more carrier wave signals to encode digital information for transmission and demodulates signals to decode the transmitted information.

Hence, the correct option is (D).

22. A light-sensitive device that converts drawing, printed text or other images into digital form is Scanner. A scanner is a device that captures images from photographic prints, posters, magazine pages, and similar sources for computer editing and display.

Hence, the correct option is (C).

23. Computer speakers or headphones are output devices. An output device is any device used to send data from a computer to another device or user. Most computer data output that is meant for humans is in the form of audio or video. Thus, most output devices used by humans are in these categories. Examples include monitors, projectors, speakers, headphones and printers.

Hence, the correct option is (D).

24. A laser printer is a popular type of personal computer printer that uses a non-impact, photocopier technology. When a document is sent to the printer, a laser beam "draws" the document on a selenium-coated drum using electrical charges. So, it is called a page printer.

Hence, the correct option is (B).

25. Joysticks typically have a button on top that is used to select the option pointed by the cursor. Joysticks are often used to control video games, and usually have one or more push-buttons whose state can also be read by the computer.

Hence, the correct option is (D).

26. Multimedia projectors of a computer are used for training presentations. A multimedia projector is a compact, high resolution, full-colour projector capable of projecting text, images, video and audio content. Typically the projector will feature inputs for a computer, DVD player, VCR, CD player and storage device.

Hence, the correct option is (B).

27. A mouse wheel is a hard plastic or rubbery disc on a computer mouse that is perpendicular to the mouse surface. It is commonly used for easy scrolling up and down through a document.

Hence, the correct option is (D).

28. The display may also be called the screen or monitor.

A display screen that provides visual output from a computer, cable box, camera or other video-generating device. The two predominant screen technologies are LCD and OLED.

Hence, the correct option is (D).

29. Joysticks are primarily used for computer gaming. These are input devices that are connected to a computer to manage game controls such as moving front, behind and sideways, shooting or other gaming tasks.

Hence, the correct option is (B).

30. An input device in computing is a piece of computer hardware equipment used to supply a data processing system including a computer or information appliance with control and data signals. Mouse, Keyboard, Scanner are examples of input devices.

Hence, the correct option is (D).

Computer Aptitude Test 15

Q.1 The work done by a computer operator is displayed in which part of computer?

A. CPU

B. VDU

C. ALU

D. Scanner

E. Motherboard

Q.2 The physical devices of a computer :

A. Software

B. Package

C. Hardware

D. System Software

E. None of these

Q.3 Which of the following allows the reuse of the software and the hardware components?

A. platform based design

B. memory design

C. peripheral design

D. input design

E. All of the above

Q.4 Reusable optical storage will typically have the acronym:

A. CD

B. RD

C. DVD

D. ROM

E. None of these

Q.5 A _________ is software, usually located at its own Web site, that lets a user specify search terms.

A. Search engine

B. Database engine

C. Meta search engine

D. Cluster

E. None of these

Q.6 A single application that combines the major features of several types of application is called as _________.

A. Integrated Software

B. A suite

C. A combo package

D. High end

E. None of these

Q.7 Software instruction intended to satisfy a user's specific processing needs are called _____.

A. system software

B. process software

C. documentation

D. application software

E. All of the above

Q.8 _________ is a set of computer programs used on a computer to help perform tasks.

A. instruction

B. Software

C. Memory

D. Processor

E. None of these

Q.9 Microsoft Word is an example of -

A. An operating system

B. A processing device

C. Application software

D. An input device

E. System software

Q.10 The 'dot matrix and 'solid font printers are examples of:

A. Line printers

B. Band printer

C. Character printer

D. Ink printers

E. Drum printers

Q.11 A software that can be freely accessed and modified.

A. Synchronous Software

B. Package Software

C. OSS

D. Middleware

E. None of these

Q.12 Which monitor would provide the highest level of performance?

A. VGA

B. XGA

C. CGA

D. SVGA

E. None of the above

Q.13 Which among the following is used for denoting the detectable movement of a computer mouse?

A. Novint

B. Mickey

C. Snipa

D. Daisy

E. None of these

Q.14 How many pins does a SIMM have?

A. 50

B. 64

C. 30 or 72

D. 168

E. 100

Q.15 Which of the following is designed to control the operations of a computer?

A. Application Software

B. System Software

C. Utility Software

D. User

E. None of these

Q.16 The two broad categories of software are_______.

A. word processing and spreadsheet

B. transaction and application

C. Windows and Mac OS

D. system and application

E. None of these

Q.17 Which of the following is not an example of system software?

A. Language Translator

B. Utility Software

C. Communication Software

D. Word Processors

E. None of these

Q.18 What does API stand for?

A. Address Programming Interface

B. Application Programming Interface

C. Accessing Peripheral through Interface
D. Address Programming Interface
E. None of these

Q.19 Which IRQ does LPT$_1$ commonly use?
A. 1   **B.** 4   **C.** 5   **D.** 7
E. 2

Q.20 How much data will a high density (HD) floppy disk hold?
A. 124 KB   **B.** 640 KB   **C.** 1.44 MB   **D.** 2.88 MB
E. 512 KB

Q.21 System software is the set of programs that enables the computer's hardware devices and _______ software to work together.
A. management   **B.** processing
C. utility   **D.** application
E. none of these

Q.22 ____ is the term used to refer to the process of two modems establishing communications with each other.
A. Interacting   **B.** Handshaking
C. Connecting   **D.** Linking
E. Pinging

Q.23 IRQ 1 is commonly assigned to:
A. It's usually open
B. System timer
C. Real time clock
D. Keyboard
E. Floppy disk controller

Q.24 __________ is designed to solve a specific problem or to do a specific task.
A. Application Software
B. System Software
C. Utility Software
D. User
E. None of these

Q.25 Identify the network hardware of a home network -
A. Access Point   **B.** NIC Card
C. Analog Modem   **D.** FireWire
E. None of these

Q.26 The users must agree to the ______ terms and agreements when they use an open source software.
A. System   **B.** License
C. Community   **D.** Programmer
E. All of these

Q.27 Which of the following can store information in the form of microscopic pits on metal disks?
A. Laser disks   **B.** Tape cassettes
C. RAM cartridge   **D.** Punched cards
E. None of these

Q.28 A device for converting handwritten impressions into coded characters & positional coordinates for input to a computer is -
A. Touch panel   **B.** Mouse
C. Wand   **D.** Writing tablet
E. None of these

Q.29 A storage system for small amounts of data is -
A. Magnetic card   **B.** Magnetic tape
C. Optical mark reader   **D.** Punched card
E. None of these

Q.30 Which among the following is not a peripheral hardware device in a computer system?
A. Keyboard   **B.** Optical Drive
C. HDD   **D.** Printer
E. None of the above

// Smart Answer Sheet //

Correct — Percentage of students who answered correctly.   **Skipped** — Percentage of students who skipped.

Q.	Ans.	Correct / Skipped	Q.	Ans.	Correct / Skipped	Q.	Ans.	Correct / Skipped	Q.	Ans.	Correct / Skipped	Q.	Ans.	Correct / Skipped	Q.	Ans.	Correct / Skipped	Q.	Ans.	Correct / Skipped
1	B	51.69 % / 40.62 %	6	A	67.0 % / 32.12 %	11	C	55.73 % / 32.76 %	16	D	50.57 % / 31.43 %	21	D	57.1 % / 35.52 %	26	B	85.29 % / 10.04 %
2	C	62.15 % / 30.88 %	7	D	40.91 % / 46.3 %	12	D	62.47 % / 30.73 %	17	D	83.48 % / 11.04 %	22	B	50.48 % / 34.19 %	27	A	63.56 % / 34.19 %
3	A	60.86 % / 38.01 %	8	B	61.43 % / 36.71 %	13	B	54.49 % / 31.18 %	18	B	78.92 % / 10.7 %	23	D	49.71 % / 39.24 %	28	D	60.69 % / 34.68 %
4	E	50.95 % / 48.41 %	9	C	45.71 % / 33.24 %	14	C	77.66 % / 18.75 %	19	D	54.33 % / 39.46 %	24	A	61.37 % / 33.22 %	29	A	54.53 % / 38.25 %
5	A	78.22 % / 15.98 %	10	C	67.78 % / 31.46 %	15	B	60.25 % / 30.71 %	20	C	44.62 % / 34.36 %	25	A	65.08 % / 33.93 %	30	C	49.58 % / 48.21 %

//Hints and Solutions//

1. The work done by a computer operator is displayed in VDU. VDU displays images generated by a computer or other electronic device. The term VDU is often used synonymously with "monitor," but it can also refer to another type of display, such as a digital projector. Visual display units may be peripheral devices or may be integrated with the other components. VDU stands for the visual display unit.

Hence, the correct option is (B).

2. Computer hardware is the physical parts or components of a computer, such as the monitor, mouse, keyboard, computer data storage, hard disk drive (HDD), graphic cards, sound cards, memory, motherboard, and so on, all of which are physical objects that are tangible.

Hence, the correct option is (C).

3. The platform design allows the reuse of the software and the hardware components in order to cope with the increasing complexity in the design of embedded systems. Platform-based design is defined in Taxonomies for the Development and Verification of Digital Systems as "an integration oriented design approach emphasizing systematic reuse, for developing complex products based upon platforms and compatible hardware and software virtual component, intended to reduce development risks costs and time to market".

Hence, the correct option is (A).

4. Reusable optical storage will typically have the acronym CD-RW. CD-RW (Compact Disc-ReWritable) is a digital optical disc storage format. A CD-RW disc is a compact disc that can be written, read arbitrarily many times, erased, and written again.

Hence, the correct option is (E).

5. A search engine is a software system that is designed to carry out web searches. They search the World Wide Web in a systematic way for particular information specified in a textual web search query. The information may be a mix of links to web pages, images, videos, infographics, articles, research papers, and other types of files.

Hence, the correct option is (A).

6. A single application that combines the major features of of several types of application is called as Integrated software. Integrated software is software for personal computers that combines the most commonly used functions of many productivity software programs into one application. E.g MS Office.

Hence, the correct option is (A).

7. Software instruction intended to satisfy a user's specific processing needs are called application software. An application is any program or group of programs, that is designed for the end-user. Applications software (also called end-user programs) include such things as database programs, word processors, Web browsers, and spreadsheets.

Hence, the correct option is (D).

8. Computer software, or simply software, is a generic term that refers to a collection of data or computer instructions that tell the computer how to work, in contrast to the physical hardware from which the system is built, that actually performs the work.

Hence, the correct option is (B).

9. Microsoft Word is an example of an application software. An application software is computer software designed to perform a group of coordinated functions, tasks, or activities for the benefit of the user.

Hence, the correct option is (C).

10. The dot matrix and solid font printers are examples of character printers. Character printers refer to those printers which print a single character at a time in place of one line at a time. These type of printers have a very slow printing speed. Most of the character printers are impact printers. These printers are outdated and rarely used now because of their slow speeds and ability to print only text characters.

Hence, the correct option is (C).

11. OSS stands for Open source software. It is software that is distributed with its source code, making it available for use, modification, and access with its original rights. Open source code is usually stored in a public repository and shared publicly. Anyone can access the repository to use the code independently.

Hence, the correct option is (C).

12. The SVGA monitor provides the highest level of performance. A Super Video Graphics Array(SVGA) monitor is an output device which uses the SVGA standard. SVGA is a video- display-standard type developed by the Video Electronics Standard Association (VESA) for IBM- PC compatible personal computers(PCs). Thus it provides highest level of performance.

Hence, the correct option is (D).

13. A mickey is a unit of measurement for the speed and movement direction of a computer mouse. So it is used for denoting the movement of a computer mouse. 1 mickey is the smallest measurable movement of a computer mouse, typically equal to 1/200th of an inch, or just over 0.1mm. The sensitivity of a computer mouse is likewise measured in mickeys-per-inch, while its speed is measured in mickeys-per-second.

Hence, the correct option is (B).

14. A SIMM, stands for Single In-line Memory Module, is a type of memory module containing random-access memory used in computers from the early 1980s to the late 1990s.It has either 30 pins or 72 pins.

Hence, the correct option is (C).

15. Software is basically classified into two: System and application. System Software is designed to control the operations and extend the processing capability of a computer system.

Hence, the correct option is (B).

16. The two broad categories of software are system and application.

There are two main types of software: systems software and application software.

Systems software includes the programs that are dedicated to managing the computer itself, such as the operating system, file management utilities, and disk operating system (or DOS).

Application software is a type of computer program that performs a specific personal, educational, and business function. Each program is designed to assist the user with a particular process, which may be related to productivity, creativity, and/or communication.

Hence, the correct option is (D).

17. A system software is responsible for controlling the operations of a computer system. Word Processor is an application software since it is specific to its purpose.

Hence, the correct option is (D).

18. API stands for Application Programming Interface. The platform-based design helps in the reuse of both the hardware and the software components. The application programming interface helps in extending the platform towards software applications.

Hence, the correct option is (B).

19. LPT_1 is use commonly IRQ 7. LPT (line print terminal) is the usual designation for a parallel port connection to a printer or other device on a personal computer. IRQs (interrupt request line) are hardware lines over which devices can send interrupt signals to the microprocessor. Below is a table of the common IRQ uses.

IRQ Level	Common Use
0	Timer
1	Keyboard
2	Cascade from IRQ 9
3	COM2 or COM4
4	COM1 or COM3
5	LPT_2
6	Floppy disk controller
7	**LPT_1**
8	Real-time clock
9	Cascade to IRQ 2
10	Unused

Hence, the correct option is (D).

20. Floppy disks are inserted in to a floppy disk drive or simply floppy drive to allow data to be read or stored. Floppy disks store much less data than a CD-ROM disk or USB flash drive. A normal 3½ inch disk can store 1.44 MB (megabytes) of data. This is usually enough for simple text documents

Hence, the correct option is (C).

21. System software is the set of programs that enables your computer's hardware devices and application software to work together. System software is software designed to provide a platform for other software.

Hence, the correct option is (D).

22. Handshaking is the term used to refer to the process of two modems establishing communications with each other. A modem handshake is what occurs when the receiving modem answers the phone call and the two modems begin to communicate.

Hence, the correct option is (B).

23. IRQ 1 is commonly assigned to Keyboard on PS/2 port. IRQ is a hardware signal sent to the processor that temporarily stops a running program and allows a special program, an interrupt handler, to run instead. Below is a table of the common IRQ uses.

IRQ Level	Common Use
0	Timer
1	**Keyboard**
2	Cascade from IRQ 9
3	COM2 or COM4
4	COM1 or COM3
5	LPT_2
6	Floppy disk controller
7	LPT_1
8	Real-time clock
9	Cascade to IRQ 2
10	Unused

Hence, the correct option is (D).

24. Application software is a type of computer program that performs a specific personal, educational, and business function. Each program is designed to assist the user with a particular process, which may be related to productivity, creativity, and/or communication.

Hence, the correct option is (A).

25. In home network access point is use. An access point is a device that creates a wireless local area network, or WLAN, usually in an office or large building. An access point connects to a wired router, switch, or hub via an Ethernet cable, and projects a Wi-Fi signal to a designated area. A wireless access point (WAP) is a networking device that allows wireless-capable devices to connect to a wired network. It is simpler and easier to install WAPs to connect all the computers or devices in your network than to use wires and cables.

Hence, the correct option is (A).

26. The users must agree to the license terms and agreement in order to access an open source software. There is a limitation of OSS that the users cannot modify the terms and conditions of any software.

Hence, the correct option is (B).

27. Laser disk scan store information in the form of microscopic pits on metal disks. Laser Disc (abbreviated as LD) is a home video format and the first commercial optical disc storage medium, initially licensed, sold and marketed as MCA DiscoVision in the United States in 1978. Although the format was capable of offering higher-quality video and audio than its consumer rivals.

Hence, the correct option is (A).

28. A Writing tablet (also known as a digitizer, drawing tablet, drawing pad, graphic tablet, digital drawing tablet, pen tablet, or

digital art board) is a computer input device that enables a user to hand-draw images, animations and graphics, with a special pen-like stylus, similar to the way a person draws images with a pencil and paper. These tablets may also be used to capture data or handwritten impressions into coded characters. It can also be used to trace an image from a piece of paper which is taped or otherwise secured to the tablet surface. Capturing data in this way, by tracing or entering the corners of linear poly-lines or shapes, is called digitizing.

Hence, the correct option is (D).

29. A storage system for small amounts of data is Magnetic card. A magnetic card is a type of card capable of storing data by modifying the magnetism of tiny iron-based magnetic particles on a band of magnetic material on the card. The magnetic stripe, sometimes called swipe card or magstripe, is read by swiping past a magnetic reading head.

Hence, the correct option is (A).

30. A HDD is a data storage device that lives inside the computer. It has spinning disks inside where data is stored magnetically. The HDD has an arm with several "heads" (transducers) that read and write data on the disk.

Peripheral device, also known as peripheral, computer peripheral, input-output device, or input/output device, any of various devices (including sensors) used to enter information and instructions into a computer for storage or processing and to deliver the processed data to a human operator or, in some cases, a machine controlled by the computer. For example:

- Monitor
- Keyboard
- Mouse
- Microphone
- Disk drive
- USB drive
- Optical drives
- Scanner
- Printer

Hence, the correct option is (C).

Q.1 Internet works on _______.
A. Packet switching
B. Circuit switching
C. Both packet switching and circuit switching
D. Pata switching
E. None of these

Q.2 DHCP (dynamic host configuration protocol) provides _______ to the client.
A. IP address
B. MAC address
C. URL
D. Both (A) and (B)
E. None of these

Q.3 IRC stands for ___.
A. Internet Resource Channel
B. Internet Routing Channels
C. Internet Rights Council
D. Internet Relay Chat
E. None of the above

Q.4 The Internet is most accurately categorized as a_________.
A. LAN
B. PAN
C. WAN
D. MAN
E. None of these

Q.5 Email works on one of the following principles, Which is the one?
A. Forward and Backward Principle
B. Store and Retrieve Principle
C. Store and Forward Principle
D. Front and Back Principle
E. None of these

Q.6 The standard protocol of the Internet is __________.
A. Flash
B. Java
C. HTML
D. TCP/IP
E. None of these

Q.7 Which of the following is not related to e-mail?
A. BCC
B. SPAM
C. Pen
D. Pine
E. None of these

Q.8 Which of the following topology share a single channel on which all station can receive and transmit?
A. Ring
B. Bus
C. Tree
D. Star
E. None of these

Q.9 When sending an e-mail, the ____ line describes the contents of the message.
A. To
B. Subject
C. Contents
D. CC
E. None of these

Q.10 Main protocol used in Internet_______.
A. X.25
B. IPX/SPX
C. TCP/IP
D. Token Bus
E. None of the above

Q.11 The network where all the nodes are around a central server is a_______.
A. Bus network
B. Star network
C. Ring network
D. Both (A) and (B)
E. None of these

Q.12 MIME is an acronym for -
A. Multiprogramming Internet Mail Extension
B. Multicasting Internet Mail Extension
C. Multiple Internet Mail Extension
D. Multipurpose Internet Mail Extension
E. None of these

Q.13 The computer jargon - WWWW, stands for :
A. World Wide Web Worm
B. World Wide Wildlife Web
C. World Wide Women's Web
D. World Wide Women's Week
E. None of these

Q.14 World Wide Web pages can be described as multimedia pages. This means that the pages may contain.
A. Text, pictures, sound
B. Text and pictures only
C. Video clips, text, pictures
D. Video clips, sound
E. All of the above

Q.15 Which of the following topology is least affected by addition/removal of a node?
A. Ring
B. Bus
C. Star
D. Mesh
E. Tree

Q.16 A host on the Internet finds another host by its ___________.
A. Postal address
B. IP address
C. Electronic Address
D. Both (A) and (B)
E. None of the above

Q.17 Which is the false statement:
A. TCP enable dataflow for monitoring
B. It avoid network saturation
C. TCP makes communication between server and client.
D. In TCP/IP model Internet layer is closest to the user.
E. All of the above

Q.18 In HTTPS, 'S' is stands for:
A. Simple
B. Secured
C. Server
D. Speed

E. None of these

Q.19 A Web site's main page is called its__________.
A. Home Page | **B.** Browser Page
C. Search Page | **D.** Bookmark
E. All of the above

Q.20 The Internet Protocol (IP) ___________.
A. Handles software computer addresses
B. Finds the quickest route between two computers
C. Ensures that connections are maintained between computers
D. Both (A) and (B)
E. None of the above

Q.21 Which of the following protocol is used for e-mail services.
A. SMAP | **B.** SMTP
C. SMIP | **D.** SMOP
E. None of these

Q.22 The size of an IP address in IPv6 is ________.
A. 32 bits | **B.** 64 bits | **C.** 128 bits | **D.** 265 bits
E. 320 bits

Q.23 In HTTP pipelining -
A. Multiple HTTP requests are sent on a single TCP connection without waiting for the corresponding responses
B. Multiple HTTP requests can not be sent on a single TCP connection
C. Multiple HTTP requests are sent in a queue on a single TCP connection
D. Both (A) and (B)
E. None of these

Q.24 Outlook Express is a _________.
A. E-Mail Client | **B.** Browser
C. Search Engine | **D.** Both (A) and (B)
E. All of the above

Q.25 Google Chrome, Mozilla , Firefox, Internet Explorer, Netscape, Navigator are examples of:
A. Web server | **B.** Web browser
C. Internet | **D.** World wide web
E. None of these

Q.26 The process of transferring files from a computer on the Internet to your computer is called?
A. Uploading | **B.** Downloading
C. FTP | **D.** JPEG
E. None of these

Q.27 Google is a____.
A. Virus Programme | **B.** Search Engine
C. Website | **D.** Hardware
E. None of these

Q.28 To reload a Web page, press the _________ button.
A. Redo | **B.** Refresh
C. Ctrl | **D.** Reload

E. All of the above

Q.29 Servers are computers that provide resources to other computers connected to a_____.
A. Supercomputer | **B.** Mainframe
C. Client | **D.** Network
E. None of these

Q.30 Which of the following is NOT a Microsoft Internet tool or technology?
A. Dreamweaver | **B.** Silverlight
C. Internet Explorer | **D.** Expression Web
E. All of the above

// Smart Answer Sheet //

Correct Percentage of students who answered correctly.   **Skipped** Percentage of students who skipped.

Q.	Ans.	Correct / Skipped	Q.	Ans.	Correct / Skipped	Q.	Ans.	Correct / Skipped	Q.	Ans.	Correct / Skipped	Q.	Ans.	Correct / Skipped	Q.	Ans.	Correct / Skipped
1	A	48.93 % / 37.6 %	6	D	88.02 % / 10.54 %	11	B	82.69 % / 14.52 %	16	B	23.84 % / 71.63 %	21	B	62.84 % / 36.05 %	26	C	65.61 % / 30.43 %
2	A	51.52 % / 35.29 %	7	C	62.75 % / 31.06 %	12	D	41.77 % / 51.37 %	17	D	63.43 % / 34.12 %	22	C	15.77 % / 82.05 %	27	B	82.51 % / 13.46 %
3	D	56.7 % / 42.63 %	8	B	88.13 % / 11.31 %	13	A	62.35 % / 30.05 %	18	B	82.78 % / 14.37 %	23	A	40.76 % / 58.24 %	28	B	68.47 % / 30.23 %
4	C	56.55 % / 33.1 %	9	B	53.63 % / 36.02 %	14	E	68.13 % / 31.56 %	19	A	80.69 % / 14.93 %	24	A	42.82 % / 31.86 %	29	D	50.49 % / 34.91 %
5	C	43.82 % / 37.13 %	10	C	43.76 % / 47.3 %	15	A	47.64 % / 46.18 %	20	A	57.66 % / 32.6 %	25	B	58.33 % / 30.72 %	30	A	59.42 % / 37.78 %

//Hints and Solutions//

1. The Internet works on packet switching. Packet switching is the way on the basis of which the Internet works. Packet switching facilitates the delivery of packets of data between devices on a shared network.

Hence the correct option is (A).

2. DHCP (dynamic host configuration protocol) provides an IP address to the client. Dynamic Host Configuration Protocol (DHCP) is a client/server protocol that automatically provides an Internet Protocol (IP) host with its IP address and other related configuration information such as the subnet mask and default gateway.

Hence the correct option is (A).

3. IRC stands for Internet Relay Chat. IRC is a multi-user, multi-channel chat system that is run on a Network. Like the telephone, the Internet allows people to communicate with each other from any place in the world at the same time.

Hence the correct option is (D).

4. The Internet is most accurately categorized as a WAN. A wide area network is a telecommunications network or computer network that extends over a large geographical distance/place. Wide area networks are often established with leased telecommunication circuits.

Hence the correct option is (C).

5. E-mail works as the sender composes a message using the email client on their computer. When the user sends the message, the email text and attachments are uploaded to the SMTP server as outgoing mail.

Hence the correct option is (C).

6. The Internet protocol suite is the conceptual model and set of communications protocols used on the Internet and similar computer networks. It is commonly known as TCP/IP because the foundational protocols in the suite are the Transmission Control Protocol (TCP) and the Internet Protocol (IP).

Hence the correct option is (D).

7. Pen is not related to e-mail. Bcc (blind carbon copy) to tertiary recipients who receive the message. Spam is unsolicited or undesired electronic messages. Pine is a freeware, text-based email client.

Hence the correct option is (C).

8. Bus topology is a network type in which every computer and network device is connected to a single channel. It transmits the data from one end to another in a single direction. It is a multi-point connection and a non-robust topology because if the backbone fails the topology crashes.

Hence the correct option is (B).

9. When sending an e-mail, the subject line describes the contents of the message.

Subject Line is an introduction that identifies the intent of the email. This subject line displayed to the email user or recipient when they look at their list of messages in their inbox should tell the recipient what the message is about, what the sender wants to convey.

Hence the correct option is (B).

10. Main protocol used in Internet TCP/IP.

It is commonly known as TCP/IP because the foundational protocols in the suite are the Transmission Control Protocol (TCP) and the Internet Protocol (IP). The Internet protocol suite is the conceptual model and set of communications protocols used on the Internet and similar computer networks. It is commonly known as TCP/IP because the foundational protocols in the suite are the Transmission Control Protocol (TCP) and the Internet Protocol (IP).

TCP/IP, or the Transmission Control Protocol/Internet Protocol, is a suite of communication protocols used to interconnect network devices on the internet. TCP/IP can also be used as a communications protocol in a private network (an intranet or an extranet).

Hence the correct option is (C).

11. In star topology, all the devices are connected to a central computer or server in a star-shaped arrangement. The central computer is known as the hub and all the nodes and devices communicate with each other through the hub; the data passes through the central server.

Hence the correct option is (B).

12. Multipurpose Internet Mail Extensions (MIME) is an Internet standard that extends the format of email to support. The MIME stands for Multi-Purpose Internet Mail Extensions. As the name indicates, it is an extension to the Internet email protocol that allows it's users to exchange different kinds of data files over the Internet such as images, audio, and video.

Hence the correct option is (D).

13. The World-Wide Web Worm (WWWW) is the first search engine for the World-Wide Web, though it was not released until March 1994, by which time a number of other search engines had been made publicly available.

It was developed in September 1993 by Oliver McBryan at the University of Colorado. The worm created a database of 300,000 multimedia objects which could be obtained or searched for keywords via the WWW. In contrast to present-day search engines, the WWWW featured support for Perl regular expressions.

Hence the correct option is (A).

14. World Wide Web pages can be described as multimedia pages. This means that the pages may contain -

Video clips, Text, pictures, sound all.

On the World Wide Web pages, we can search every thing that we want to know.

Hence the correct option is (E).

15. Ring topology is least affected by the addition/removal of a node. Ring topologies are connected to each other node in a circle, so it is least affected by addition or removal.

Hence the correct option is (A).

16. A host on the internet finds another host by its IP Address. An Internet Protocol address (IP address) is a numerical label assigned to each device connected to a computer network that uses the Internet Protocol for communication An IP address serves two main functions: host or network interface identification and location addressing.

Hence the correct option is (B).

17. There is no internet layer in the TCP/IP model. In the OSI model, the internet layer is the layer that is the "closest to the end-user". The full name of TCP/IP is Transmission Control Protocol/Internet Protocol. It is a set of rules that decide how the Internet works. TCP/IP is used in real environments, TCP/IP is a protocol of world-wide-web (www) which we call the Internet. All networks and protocols work on the TCP/IP model.

Hence the correct option is (D).

18. HTTPS stands for HyperText Transfer Protocol Secure (HTTPS) is the secure version of HTTP, the protocol over which data is sent between your browser and the website that you are connected to.

Hence the correct option is (B).

19. A home page or a start page is the initial or main web page of a website or a browser. The initial page of a website is sometimes called main page as well.

Hence the correct option is (A).

20. The Internet Protocol (IP) handles software computer addresses. The Internet Protocol (IP) is a protocol, or set of rules, for routing and addressing packets of data so that they can travel across networks and arrive at the correct destination. IP information is attached to each packet, and this information helps routers to send packets to the right place.

Hence the correct option is (A).

21. SMTP is the protocol used for e-mail services. SMTP stands for Simple Mail Transfer Protocol. SMTP is a set of communication guidelines that allow software to transmit electronic mail over the Internet, it is called Simple Mail Transfer Protocol. It is a program used to send messages to other computer users based on e-mail addresses.

Hence the correct option is (B).

22. An IPv6 address is 128 bits long. Therefore, 2128 i.e. 340 undecillion addresses are possible in IPv6. IPv4 has only 4 billion possible addresses and IPv6 would be a brilliant alternative in case IPv4 runs out of possible new addresses.

Hence the correct option is (C).

23. In HTTP pipelining, multiple HTTP requests are sent on a single TCP connection without waiting for the corresponding responses.

HTTP pipelining helps the client make multiple requests without having to waiting for each response, thus saving a lot of time and bandwidth for the client.

Hence the correct option is (A).

24. Outlook Express is a E-Mail Client. Outlook Express, formerly known as Microsoft Internet Mail and News, is a discontinued email and news client.

Hence the correct option is (A).

25. Google Chrome, Mozilla , Firefox, Internet Explorer, Netscape, Navigator are examples of web browser.

Hence the correct option is (B).

26. The process of transferring files from a computer on the Internet to your computer is called FTP.

Uploading is the transmission of a file from one computer system to another, usually larger computer system. From an Internet user's point of view, downloading is receiving a file from another computer. The File Transfer Protocol (FTP) is the Internet facility for downloading and uploading files.

Hence the correct option is (B).

27. Google is a fully automated search engine that uses software known as "web crawlers" that explore the web on a regular basis to find sites to add to our index. In fact, the vast majority of sites listed in our results aren't manually submitted for inclusion but are found and added automatically when our web crawlers crawl the web.

Hence the correct option is (B).

28. In general, refresh is another way of describing the process of reloading or updating what is being displayed or stored.Pressing the F5 function key can refresh the Windows desktop screen. On a Mac, pressing Command+R will refresh the page you are currently viewing.

Hence the correct option is (B).

29. Servers are computers that provide resources to other computers connected to a network.Because servers can't communicate with other computers without being connected within a network may it be any.

Hence the correct option is (D).

30. Adobe Dreamweaver is a software program for designing web pages, essentially a more fully featured HTML web and programming editor. It's not a internet tool or technology.

Hence the correct option is (A).

// Notes //

// Notes //